THE PERFECT
SEARCH

THE PERFECT
SEARCH

What Every Nonprofit Board Member
Needs to Know About Hiring
Their Next CEO

Tommy W. Thomas

with
Nick Isbister and Robert C. Andringa

The Perfect Search

Copyright © 2008 by Tommy W. Thomas

Published in the United States by Credo House Publishers,
a division of Credo Communications, LLC, Grand Rapids, Michigan.
www.credocommunications.net

ISBN-13: 978-0-9787620-9-4
ISBN-10: 0-9787620-9-6

For reasons of client confidentiality and sensitivity, pseudonyms
and generalities have been used to obscure the names of individuals
and clients.

Many thanks to Bob Andringa for his thoughts on evaluating the
chief executive officer that comprise Chapter 15.

Editor: Kate Etue
Cover design: Paul Gant
Interior design: Sharon VanLoozenoord

Printed in The United States of America

10 9 8 7 6 5 4 3 2 1

First Edition

This book is dedicated to the many clients and candidates who have been a part of all the searches that we have done for not-for-profit organizations. We are grateful to our clients for asking us to participate in the future of their organizations by assisting them in the selection of their next chief executive officer. They could have worked with other consultants, but they choose us. We are grateful to all of the men and women who have been candidates for these searches. Over the years, we have worked with some of the great leaders of the not-for-profit sector in the United States. It is no wonder that the not-for-profit sector has such a significant impact in the United States.

Table of Contents

Appendices

Preface

At no previous time in the history of America has there been a bigger need or call for not-for-profit organizations to take more of a leadership role in solving some of our nation's social, moral, and economic problems. Additionally, there has never been a time when so many people, who have had successful careers in the private sector, have the opportunity to either take early retirement or otherwise give serious consideration to transitioning their careers to leadership roles with not-for-profit organizations. And finally, as not-for-profit organizations proliferate, more people from education, government, and the private sector are serving on boards of nonprofits.

In the United States alone there are nearly 2 million not-for-profit organizations. Yet, the majority are very small and sometimes do not have a full-time, salaried chief executive officer. Assuming, however, that five hundred thousand do have professional CEOs, and that the average tenure might be seven or eight years, that means there are more than sixty thousand searches going on every year!

In light of these three factors, plus the normal rate of turnover in the leadership of nonprofits, there is a tremendous need for instruction in how to correctly select the chief executive officer for this unique type of organization. All too often these decisions are made behind closed doors by a small group of people who have not taken the time to study their organization and determine what kind of leadership it needs at that time in its life. Board members need to realize that selecting their next chief executive officer is serious business, and the decision needs to be approached and executed in a manner that will provide the results they need to move their organization further toward its goals and objectives.

This book grew out of our combined sixty-plus years of consulting with boards of not-for-profit organizations.

During that time we have been involved with more than eighty nonprofit senior leadership searches, having personally interviewed more than five hundred candidates in the identification and selection of new chief executive officers for various organizations. Co-author Bob Andringa has also been involved in succession planning and the executive transition process in the change of chief executive officers at several not-for-profit organizations. Co-author Nick Isbister has served as an executive coach for several nonprofit executives in the United Kingdom.

While most people are not brought onto boards specifically to serve on their search committee, if you serve long enough or on enough boards eventually an organization you're with will go through a change of leadership, and you may be asked to serve on the search committee for a new chief executive officer. Whether the organization is a museum, a social services agency, a health and human services agency, an institution of higher education, or a religious organization, the people involved in selecting new senior leadership generally face the same challenges and have the same questions.

As consultants, we have learned much from our clients over the years. We have worked for the boards of some of the largest not-for-profit organizations in the world, and we have been involved with the initial financial backers of "fledgling start-ups," working with their boards to recruit the organization's initial leaders. We have observed some of the best "best practices" in the industry, and we have also learned "how "not to do it." Unlike scientists who spend years in a laboratory discovering the secret components of a successful formula, we have learned that identifying and recruiting a chief executive officer for a not-for-profit organization is not a formulaic process. A "one size fits all" application doesn't work here.

In this book we hope to accomplish three things. First, if you're considering whether to serve on a search committee, we want to help you make an accurate evaluation of your time and personal giftedness in light of the search committee's needs. Few things are more frustrating or detrimental to the search process than relying on people who do not or cannot commit the time required to make a meaningful contribution to the search process.

Next, we want to expose some of the pitfalls that every person serving on a search committee will face. Someone once said that serving on a search committee is like walking through a field laced with land mines. You don't always know what your next step should be. In all probability, the most important decision you will be asked to make as a board member for a not-for-profit organization is the selection of the chief executive officer. Anyone who has had this responsibility knows its challenge. Finding the right person is seldom easy. The process is time consuming. The outcome offers no guarantees. Under the best of circumstances, it's a time-intensive, calculated risk. Under the worst, it's a tiresome undertaking, riddled with unknown factors, unrelenting pressures, and unfavorable odds. We know that you can never totally eliminate all of the risks associated with the hiring process, but there are certain steps you can take to significantly reduce this risk.

Finally, we want to share some best practices we have learned from our clients over the years. Any honest consultant will tell you that it takes a certain set of skills and abilities to be one, but that what it takes to excel is honing those skills by working with and alongside your clients.

We have not set out to write a complete manual on the not-for-profit organization executive search process; rather, we seek to engage you in a thought process that, should you choose to be a member of a senior-leadership search committee, you will be further along the learning curve, armed with some good principles and processes to utilize.

In other words, this is primarily a practitioner's book: written for those men and women who are asked to serve on a search committee. It's aim is to inform you of the enormity

of your charge and to give you guidelines that will produce
the results your board is expecting and your organization
deserves.

On the pages that follow, we will discuss in depth the
search process and several areas that you should consider
when you are asked to make a hiring decision. Our hope is
that you will read this book with pencil in hand. Compare
and contrast our advice with your specific situation, and collaborate with your fellow committee members to do what is
best for your organization.

(Note: The top leadership position in a not-for-profit
organization goes by many titles. Among these are president,
executive director, chief executive officer, and so on. In this
book we are using the term "chief executive officer" to indicate the top paid leadership position in the organization, typically the only person who reports to the board of directors.)

Acknowledgments

It was a cold February day in 1995. I received a call from Rick Wellock, an organizational development consultant friend of mine from Pittsburgh. He had a client who needed an executive director for one of his not-for-profit organizations and wanted to know if I would team with him to do the search. His client was Howard Butt, Chairman of the Board of the H. E. Butt Foundation. Mr. Butt hired us to do that search, and little did I know that my career was about to change directions and move into the area of recruiting chief executives for a wide variety of not-for-profit organizations. So initial thanks go to Rick Wellock and Howard Butt.

Since then I have been involved in leading over 150 chief executive officer searches for not-for-profit organizations. To the many people who have made this career possible, the words "thank you" is hardly sufficient.

> Rob Stevenson, one of my business partners, has worked with me on many of these searches, and were it not for him, this book would not be possible. He and I have traveled the United States together, and I have learned so much from him, not only about the search business, but also human relations and life in general.

> Jim Bere and the 1997 Board of Directors of World Vision: These people entrusted me and Rob to lead the search that brought Rich Stearns to that organization after Bob Sieple retired. That was ten years ago, and we still receive several calls a month wanting to know if we were the people who did that search. If Mr. Butt launched my career, the Board of World Vision propelled it to a higher level.

> Bob Briner: Bob called one day and asked if I had ever done a college president search. I told him no, but I

was sure I could if he would give me the chance. He invited me and Rob to make a presentation to the board of a small liberal arts college. We successfully completed that search, and today recruiting college and university presidents has become a mainstay of my practice.

❯ Nick Isbister and Bob Andringa: Not only have these two men made significant contributions to this book, they have taught me a lot about consulting. They are both pros at their niche in management consulting.

❯ Fred Williams: Fred is one of the best commercial real estate attorneys I know. He represented me well when I was trying to make a go of it in commercial real estate. Perhaps his best counsel was when he called one day and said the following: "Tommy, this recession will go away one day and we will all make a lot of money in commercial real estate again . . . I just don't know when. So, my counsel to you is that if you have anything else that you want to do with the rest of your life I suggest you move on." That was the impetus I needed to think about getting out of real estate, and it ultimately led me to the executive search business.

❯ Bob Petty: In 1988 I was leaving commercial real estate and Bob Petty hired me as a rookie search consultant at Questar Partners. I remember him looking me in the eye and saying, "You certainly don't have any experience in this industry, but I will role the dice on you. I will pay all your expenses, give you half of the fees that you generate, and teach you everything I know." On all three promises, Bob was true to his word, and I am thankful that he "rolled the dice on me."

❯ Professor M. A. Honnell: After high school I enrolled at Auburn University in the College of Engineering.

Studying engineering (and ultimately graduating) was one of the most difficult things that I have ever done. There were many days when I wanted to drop out or change majors. But there was one professor who consistently encouraged me and all of the struggling students in Electrical Engineering at Auburn. From his perch by the blackboard in the front of the class, Professor Honnell could see the look of confusion or discouragement in our eyes. I can still hear him when he would say, "You fellas can do this. You are good engineers. You can compete with those guys from Georgia Tech. You can solve any engineering problem I put in front of you. Just wait 'til you graduate. You'll see." Were it not for Professor Honnell, I don't think I would have a degree in Electrical Engineering from Auburn and have no idea where my career path would have taken me.

> My wife, Nancy: She has believed in me during the discouraging times of my career. She is a great companion. She has provided a comfortable home and great cooking. She has loved me when I was unlovable. Like Professor Honnell, she continues to tell me that I can do it and that I can compete with the best of them. She has spent a lot of nights alone in Nashville while I was at a board meeting or taking a candidate to dinner in another city. I love you, Mite!

Introduction

WHO IS THE CHIEF EXECUTIVE OFFICER
OF YOUR NONPROFIT?

If you are on the board of a national nonprofit or a local or regional nonprofit which has some longevity, this may be total review for you and you can skip it. But if you serve on the board of a fairly new nonprofit, or if there seems to be confusion in your organization about who is the chief executive officer, then you should definitely read this chapter.

Don't let the title fool you. In many nonprofits, especially those which are new, small, or depend primarily on volunteer leadership, it may not be clear whether any one person has authority as the "chief executive officer." This is usually a full-time, paid staff member. But it could be a part-time volunteer in certain circumstances. Is everyone clear who your CEO is?

Reasons Why Every Nonprofit Should Designate a Chief Executive Officer

> The board of trustees or directors needs one agent to implement policy.

> Most people agree that is difficult to run a company or organization by committee. It just doesn't work. In a well-run nonprofit, the board needs one person to whom they look to implement policy.

> The board needs a chief executive officer to work with its chairman on board development.

> Good boards don't just happen. It takes hard and focused work on the part of the chief executive officer to develop a not-for-profit board into one that really works and is more than just a board in name only.

> The CEO should take the lead in the strategic planning process.

> Staff, whether paid or volunteer, need the security of knowing who's in charge.

> Donors feel confident when they know "who is running the place."

> Vendors, banks, insurance agents, and so on often want to "talk to the boss." By the same token, these people like to know that the person they are dealing with has the authority to make the decisions necessary to execute the deal.

> A clearly designated chief executive officer reduces competition, end runs, and confusion.

> If there is no one person in the organization designated as chief executive officer there is a very strong temptation for staff to go to whomever they feel they have the most chance for success with for approval of their projects, plans, and programs. This makes for a chaotic situation. A strong chief executive officer will put a stop to this behavior and establish guidelines as to who has approval for what levels of projects, programs, and so on.

> The organization needs a primary "spokesman" who articulates the mission clearly.

> Our experience in the higher education arena is that "no one can tell the story like the president." This is true not only for colleges and universities but for any not-for-profit organization. Often a staff member or officer can do their best, but every organization needs a primary spokesperson whose responsibility it is to credibly and clearly articulate the mission of the organization.

> One CEO can be held accountable to get decisions made in a timely fashion.

Accountability is key to the success of any not-for-profit organization. Someone has to take responsibility and be held accountable for decisions being made and plans and programs being executed. Obviously this goes on at all levels of the organization, but the chief executive officer is ultimately the one whom the board holds accountable.

Points for Discussion

1. Has there been confusion about who is accountable for fulfilling board policy in your organization?

2. Is it reasonable in your organization to have a volunteer "chief executive officer?"

3. Could your chief paid staff person function as the chief executive officer, given clear board policies that set the goals and define the parameters of executive action?

4. If you choose not to designate a CEO, is there a clear process of delegation about which the entire board and staff are comfortable?

5. If you are not ready to designate your top paid staff person as the chief executive officer, what conditions would need to be met for that to happen in the future?

6. Is it reasonable for a volunteer to give almost daily attention to the details of the organization's office? And is this person willing to be accountable to the board for implementation of the board's policies, having the chief paid staff person report to this volunteer CEO?

Why Do People Make Such Poor Hiring Decisions?

> **The failure to plan ahead**

> **Lack of understanding about job "fit"**

> **Poor selection process**

As many as 20 percent of chief executive officers who leave their jobs were asked by their board to do so. My experience is that, when this happens, most board members will acknowledge that "we waited too long to force a change."

Why are there so many regrettable hiring decisions about people at the chief executive officer level in not-for-profit organizations?

THE FAILURE TO PLAN AHEAD

In an ideal world the transition from one not-for-profit CEO to the next would be seamless. The outgoing leader would give the board several months' notice of her anticipated departure. She would agree to stay with the company until her replacement has been selected—a process that, on average, takes four to six months—and then would participate in a planned and orderly transition process.

One of the smoothest transitions I have ever been a part of was when an outgoing chief executive officer alerted his board that he felt his contribution to the organization had

come to a close and it was time for him to go. He told the board that he would like to leave within a year but was open to staying as long as fifteen months if necessary. The search was completed in ten months, and the incumbent remained on the job for a couple of months to aid in the transition. As a result the organization was able to have a very smooth transition between chief executive officers.

Unfortunately, we don't live in an ideal world. All too often the chief executive officer makes an unexpected departure:

> Sometimes the incumbent isn't getting the job done and the board chooses to let the person go.

> It is more often the case that the incumbent gets an offer from another organization. In some cases she will give the board ample notice of her anticipated departure, but in many cases, she will give a standard notice (often thirty days) and immediately begin her transition.

> Tragically, I have seen cases where the incumbent unexpectedly died or incurred a debilitating disease while in office.

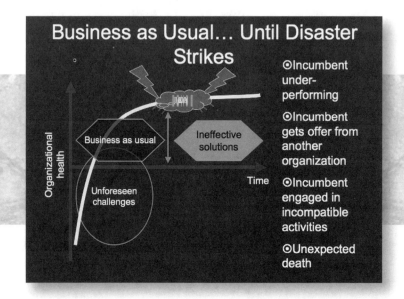

Our experience has been that, all too often, not-for-profit organizations wait until there is a vacancy in the chief executive officer position to discuss how they should proceed in their quest for a successor. This often causes a delay of several weeks or months and results in uncertainty on the part of staff, donors, and other constituents. It is much better to plan ahead when there is ample time to consider the best options.

Bob Andringa suggests that all nonprofits have a transition policy in place. The questions you need to be address to develop this plan include:

1. Is there a natural-acting CEO should something happen to ours?
2. If not, what would we do if we were suddenly faced with a vacancy?
3. Should we consider hiring a successor CEO a year or two in advance?
4. What are the issues that the board should anticipate when the current CEO leaves?
5. How will the search committee be appointed, and should we use an outside search firm?
6. What are the needs and who could help the outgoing or incoming CEO and the families involved during their transition periods?

This level of planning is not that prevalent in the not-for-profit arena, and the lack thereof contributes to poor, delayed transitions and ultimately poor hiring decisions. It is our opinion that after appropriate review by key stakeholders, the board should adopt a policy to keep on file in case search becomes necessary. This makes for a much smoother transition.

LACK OF UNDERSTANDING ABOUT JOB FIT

Being fully engaged in one's work and feeling fulfilled by one's efforts are two highly critical criteria for both employee

performance and retention. Gallup Research studies report that people who have the opportunity to use their natural or "innate" strengths every day are *six times* as likely to be engaged in their work. In addition, these people are more than *three times* as likely to report having an excellent quality of life in general.[1]

Why then do so many decision makers in all kinds of organizations fail to use these well-known facts as the basis for making more informed hiring and promotion decisions?

Part of the problem lies in the myths our twentieth-century culture has taught us about people and human behavior. Probably the most powerful myth that has a strangle-hold on organizational culture is the misguided maxim that "You can be anything you want to be, if you work hard enough."

Because our culture is so strongly based on the premise of equal opportunity, most people readily embrace this "be anything you want to be" concept. Basing their thinking on this premise, they make further erroneous assumptions that performance can be "developed" with incentives, training, and feedback. The fact that people cannot really "change their spots or their stripes" is lost in the promise of what they believe is to come.

However, anyone who has worked with or supervised others has quickly learned that people do not change their natural or "motivated" behaviors. (Parents, and some more quickly than others, learn this about their children as well.)

> The manager who is highly directive and tells his employees precisely how he wants a task performed does not suddenly (or even over time) become consistently "facilitative."

> Executives who have strong "private vision" do not sustain collaborative, grassroots, consensus behaviors, even with benefit of the most prestigious executive development programs.

> Most importantly, both of these individuals could be powerful, effective performers in roles that required their respective strengths.

Sadly for all concerned, organizations continue to invest billions in resources trying to "develop" their leaders to fit a job that doesn't match their natural talents or gifts. Meanwhile, little or no effort is spent trying to determine what the person is naturally motivated to do—and whether or not those motivations "fit" the critical requirements of the job and role under consideration.

Some prominent management gurus are beginning to recognize the importance of fit to job performance and employee retention. In his best-selling book, author Jim Collins reports that we move from *Good to Great* by getting "the right people in the right seats."[2] Unfortunately, Mr. Collins does not tell the reader how to determine whether a person is "right" for a given seat.

This lack of methodology for identifying natural strengths as the basis for job fit is a significant and pervasive problem that *The Perfect Search* can correct. Using a unique assessment, you can gather and interpret recurring *evidence* that identifies a candidate's natural strengths and accurately *predicts* a candidate's performance in a specific job role. This assessment can also be used to define the critical requirements for performing a role, thus providing a sound basis for "matching" the person to the job. (This process is explained more fully in Chapter 4.)

> Little or no effort is spent trying to determine what the person is naturally motivated to do—and whether or not those motivations "fit" the critical requirements of the job and role under consideration.

POOR SELECTION PROCESS

If you have served on many boards, you have probably observed a wide variety of poor selection-process habits. Among these are:

> Rushing through the selection process
> Promoting the senior person with the longest time of service. Why? Because he has been loyal to the organization and there would be little disruption during the transition
> Hiring a relative of one of the board members, or a board member who volunteers to take over for very little salary
> Hiring one of the large donors to the organization

Many poor selection processes happen because adequate time is not given to thinking through the kind of leader the organization needs at that moment in the organization's life cycle.

Later in the book I will share my opinions on how incorrect beliefs about people impact the hiring process. However, I will spend considerably more time sharing how to do a search that is not rushed.

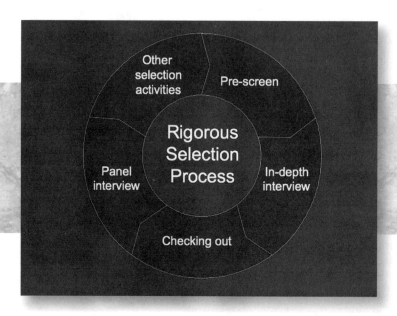

Preparing for
the Perfect Search

2

> Developing a board policy

> The perfect search

An effective search for your next chief executive officer does not happen without proper preparation and hard work in executing the plan. The seeds for an effective search are best planted months, if not years, in advance of the actual search.

As I mentioned in Chapter 1, it is my opinion that not-for-profit boards should develop in advance a board policy that details what should happen when the time comes to search for a new chief executive officer. Once this policy is determined, it can be filed and implemented when needed. In creating this document the board can prevent hasty and perhaps premature actions, or other rash decisions that often occur when unprepared for the inevitable—selecting a new chief executive officer.

> An effective search for your next chief executive officer does not happen without proper preparation and hard work in executing the plan.

DEVELOPING A BOARD POLICY

Although this policy can be amended for unusual situations, I highly recommend that the board consider these key issues when creating their particular policy:

The Acting Chief Executive Officer

> ❯ If the CEO vacancy occurs immediately, as a surprise, who should be named acting CEO the next day?

> ❯ Should this person, usually a senior staff person, be paid the same as the CEO was paid?

> ❯ Assuming there are reasons to look for someone to serve for up to a year or two as interim, is it appropriate to make that decision now?

The Interim Chief Executive Officer

> ❯ If needed, how is the interim chief executive officer to be selected?

> ❯ How long should she expect to serve?

> ❯ Will the interim chief executive officer be eligible as a candidate for the permanent position?

> ❯ How will the interim chief executive officer be compensated?

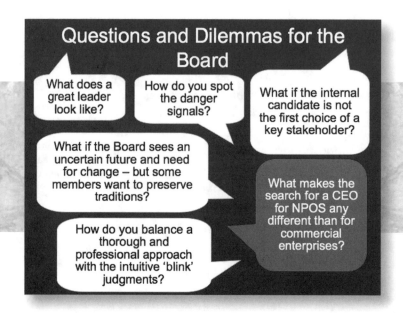

The Search and Selection Committee

> ❯ Will you have a search committee and a selection committee, or will one committee handle both functions?

> ❯ How many people will serve on your search committee?

> ❯ What groups of constituents (other than board members) should be represented on the search committee?

> ❯ Who will appoint the non-board members?

> ❯ Who will chair the search committee?

> ❯ Will a search consultant be retained, and if so by whom?

> ❯ What is the best way to utilize the services of a search consultant?

> ❯ What is the board's charge to the search committee? To bring their top candidate, or the top two or three, rank ordered?

> ❯ What will be the budget for the search?

Staff Support for the Search

> ❯ Will someone on staff serve as a liaison to the search committee?

> ❯ If so, how much time should this person be expected to spend on search-related activities?

> ❯ How will the confidential issues and areas of the search be kept confidential?

Transition Issues of Concern to the Board

> ❯ What length of time, if any, should the outgoing chief executive officer overlap with the incoming chief executive officer, if that's even possible?

> Will the outgoing chief executive officer receive emeritus status?

> What is the best way to introduce the new chief executive officer to the constituents?

> Should you appoint a transition committee to oversee the transition from one CEO to the next?

Base-lining the New Chief Executive Officer's Compensation Package

> What correlation should there be between the outgoing chief executive officer's compensation and the incoming chief executive officer's compensation?

> What role will compensation surveys play in the determining of the new chief executive officer's salary?

> Should the board use a compensation consultant to assist in determining the salary range or level?

Fair Treatment of the Outgoing Chief Executive Officer

> Should the outgoing chief executive officer remain on the Board of Directors or Trustees? If not, what role or relationship should she have with the board?

> What are the pros and cons of the board retaining the outgoing chief executive officer for limited paid roles?

> Should you appoint a committee to handle the transition from one chief executive officer to the next?

Some of the above questions seem obvious. The remainder is certainly not rocket science, yet you would be surprised at the number of nonprofit boards who find themselves unprepared facing the selection of their next leader. Many of these issues will also be addressed in the subsequent chapters.

THE PERFECT SEARCH

After fifteen years in the business, I'm still not sure I have ever been part of a "perfect search." But when I think of some of the best searches that I have been privileged to be a part of, certain words and phrases come to mind. Giving due consideration to these concepts is a large part of preparing for a successful search process.

Balance

Searches seem to go most smoothly when there is balance in the composition of the search committee, which can take several forms:

Balance in the representation of the stakeholders. When your selection team is balanced in the representation of the organization's stakeholders, you are more likely to have buy-in and ownership of both the process and its outcome. When a search committee does not have this balance, it is common to complete the process and then have one or more constituent groups, rightly or wrongly, come forward and question the process. This can cause major turmoil as well as wasted time.

Balance between patience and persistence. While everyone wants the search to be completed as quickly as possible, there are certain aspects of the process that should not be rushed or skipped. Occasionally people will want to do too many things simultaneously, which usually has a negative impact upon the outcome. The best search committees I have worked with have been those which, before starting, have a realistic understanding of the amount of time—personally and corporately—the search is going to take to truly benefit the organization.

The vast majority of the executive searches I have conducted have had a fairly tight timeline. In many cases it seemed that the board "wanted it completed yesterday." By the same token, most of these people did not want to sacrifice quality for expediency. Those who were willing to wait found that the right person came to the forefront.

While every person involved in the search must be persistent in doing their assigned tasks, they must also be patient and allow the process to work.

Balance between realism and high standards or aspirations. There is a natural tension between realism and having high standards or aspirations. One story that makes its rounds in the lore of consultants such as myself is that of the search for a chief executive officer at a large metropolitan museum. The museum's search committee wanted an individual with proven expertise in curatorship and management, with a master's degree in business administration and a doctorate in Art History. As the story goes, "At last count, there were only five such individuals in the United States." Limiting your executive search to a pool of five candidates will rarely produce a good fit for the organization. And while you certainly do not want to compromise your standards on what you want in your next chief executive officer, this must be tempered with a touch of realism.

Balance in the natural talents or gifts of the search committee members. "Balance" on search committees is often defined in terms of the personality or temperament of each of its members. I prefer to address the issue of balance in terms of how people are naturally gifted or wired to perform their tasks and roles. To better understand the nature and range of motivations commonly present in committee members, I find it is useful to contrast typical performance behaviors. Consider the following:

> Some people are naturally gifted to focus on the long-range or "big picture" issues; others delve into short-term action items and details.

> Some people bring strong "private visions" to the table—which may or may not be appropriate for the given mission and objectives of the committee. Other members are motivated to work collaboratively to involve others in building a consensus vision.

> Some people are gifted at recognizing the value or potential in an idea or opportunity; others are more motivated to assess the risk or downside.

> Some people are motivated to develop strategies from a somewhat ambiguous objective; others require clear directions or requirements in order to proceed.

> Some people understand the importance of process and are motivated to participate in and contribute to that process; others are more goal-oriented and may want to move quickly to solutions and actions items.

> Some people seek specific measurable results (such as customer satisfaction, continuous improvement, or profitability) as outcomes for their efforts. Others seek results that are less measurable (such as effectiveness, ethics, or goodwill).

> Some individuals are highly proactive and will move forward without requiring support or cues from other members or the facilitator. Others show initiative only under select circumstances and will take action only after some other condition has been established.

The moral of this story is that all of these people bring useful and necessary motivations to the table. The challenge is to assemble the right balance of "gifts" for the specific nature of the task for which the committee has been convened.

Perspective

For a committee to hold a successful search for its new chief executive officer, its members must have proper perspective, which exhibits itself in the following ways:

Search committee members want to serve and understand the cost of being a good committee member. Occasionally you will find people who really don't want to be on a search committee serving only because someone coerced them into it. I have also seen members of a committee fail to really think

through the time commitment, and they ended up unavailable during critical times of the search. Both of these situations can be detrimental to the process.

The committee has realistic salary limitations. The prudent search committee will have to live with the tensions and realities of their organization's salary limitations. Every organization has a realistic ceiling for compensation. Occasionally one of my not-for-profit clients asks me to find them a "dollar a year" chief executive officer, one that essentially works for free in their "retirement" years. Usually they say this in jest but wonder if their organization might be so lucky as to find one of these people. In rare instances I have succeeded in finding just that type of candidate, however read Appendix A for more on the downsides of this type of leader.

One way of getting around any salary limitations your organization may have is to allow the chief executive officer to have a limited number of days a year where she is allowed to consult with other organizations. This gives your chief executive officer the opportunity to generate additional income, but it also means that she may bring some new ideas and approaches to your organization as a result of her other work.

Flexibility, When Appropriate

A good search committee will maintain a flexible attitude toward their requirements, as long as it is appropriate. Compromise on non-essentials can aid in securing the best possible candidate for the position.

The committee understands the location requirements for the job. In our changing world, a few not-for-profit organizations are finding that their chief executive officers do not necessarily have to reside in the vicinity of the headquarters, however in the great majority of cases the chief executive officer will have to live near the work of the organization.

I once worked on a search in which the organization's headquarters and home office was in Chicago. The board expected its new chief executive officer to average at least two days a week at the headquarters and preferred that he reside in the Chicago area. However, they realized that for the caliber of person they wanted, this might mean allowing the person to work out some sort of commuting arrangement instead of relocating. In the end, the board realized that the position required the executive to travel 30 to 40 percent of the time anyway, so they figured this compromise was fair.

In contrast, a liberal arts college in the northeastern United States was looking for a new president, but they were located in a rather remote area. One member of the search committee asked, "What are you going to do about the location?" I responded that there wasn't anything I could do about it. For this type of position, the person would need to live near the campus. If they selected me to do their search, I would find candidates who were naturally drawn to live in that area of the country.

The committee understands the job requirements. Unrealistic expectations can destroy a search. I am not suggesting that you settle for second best or not "reach for the stars" when

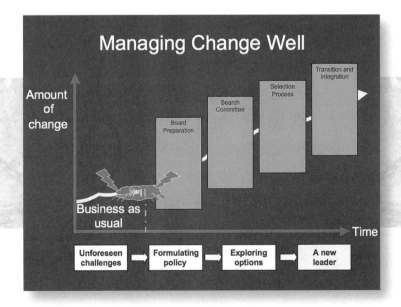

you dream of the next leader for your organization; however experience has taught me to temper my hopes and dreams with a bit of realism. But sometimes you can find exactly what you're looking for when you stand by your convictions.

Early in my career, the search firm I was employed by was retained by a British-Japanese joint venture to find a Managing Director for their operation, which would be located in Tokyo. Critical requirements aside, the experience and other qualifications for the position were extreme: The job was located in Tokyo. The individual had to read, write, and speak English and Japanese and be comfortable living in Japan. The desired undergraduate degree was Mechanical Engineering with an MBA from a top United States business school. The candidate needed to have worked in engineering as well as finance. To top it off, the person could be neither British nor Japanese, because the British did not trust their Japanese partners, and the Japanese did not trust their British partners.

As you might imagine the pool of qualified candidates was very small. In the end there were only three people we were able to find who met the requirements. The client was pleased with the pool and ultimately hired a young man who was Peruvian, had been raised in Japan, got his Mechanical Engineering degree from the University of California-Berkeley, took his MBA from the University of Pennsylvania's The Wharton School and did his early career work in the design and construction of Disney-Japan! By sticking to their initial job requirements rather than compromising, the board was able to find a person with the exact requirements they desired.

Strong Administrative Assistance

Every search needs someone with strong administrative skills who has time to devote to the many administrative and follow-up activities of a search. This must be someone who has the confidence of the members of the search committee because ultimately this person will be handling a lot of highly confidential material.

I have worked on searches where the administrative needs were generally handled in the one of the following ways.

> A part time person who is present at all committee meetings and works closely with the Chair of the Search Committee and the consultant (if one is used)

> A member of the Search Committee who has these skills is often asked to serve in this capacity. This alleviates the need for a part-time person, but it really can put a strain on the committee member's time, especially toward the end of the search when a lot of details and logistics seem to hit at once.

> The administrative assistant to the Chair of the Search Committee is asked by her boss to serve in this capacity. In this case, the person wasn't always at all the meetings, but because of the nature of their working relationship, was always in close communication with the Chair.

As I stated at the beginning of this chapter, I have not worked on that many perfect searches, but I always counsel my clients to do their best to strive to be close to perfect. You will not always get it right, but striving to get it right in these areas will get you off to a good start:

> Balance
> Perspective
> Flexibility
> Strong Administrative Assistance

The Search Committee

3

> Values common to each member of the search committee

> Before you agree to serve on a search committee

> Determining the size and composition of the search committee

> Who should chair the search committee?

> Qualities of effective search committee members

Serving on the search committee for your favorite charity or nonprofit can be a very rewarding experience. Most people derive a lot of satisfaction from helping to bring a new leader into an organization and looking back in a few years to celebrate this person's success.

VALUES COMMON TO EACH MEMBER OF THE SEARCH COMMITTEE

While it's important to balance your search committee with varying personality types, areas of giftedness, and character strengths, it's also wise to make some generalizations about the values you want to see in *each* member of the search committee.

Participation

An effective search committee is one where each member makes a valuable contribution to the process. You don't want

someone who comes to the meetings but does not partici-
pate. Part of the reason for having a committee, rather than
one person, make this decision is the outcome you get when
members of the committee participate and collaborate.

Transparency

This can be a bit tricky because many people are not naturally transparent. Some people choose to keep their thoughts
to themselves, particularly if their thoughts run contrary to
those of the group. In an ideal world, you don't want many of
these people on the committee. You need those who will contribute to the success of the search process by voicing their
opinions, even when they are contrary to the thinking of the
group. Ultimately you want to build consensus, but consensus usually begins with a variety of ideas and opinions.

Spirit of Collaboration

The best searches are those whose committee members "trust
the process." These men and women realize that collaboration
will take them further and faster toward the goal of getting
the right chief executive officer than working individually as
"lone rangers" will.

BEFORE YOU AGREE TO SERVE ON A SEARCH COMMITTEE

Serving on a search committee can be a very time-consuming
task. Hiring a new leader is a very important decision in the life
of any organization, and it deserves the greatest degree of concern and attention from all members of the search committee.

Before agreeing to serve, make sure you can willingly give
the time and attention required. In addition to the periodic
meetings you will need to attend, pay particular attention
to the time it will take to adequately interview the finalists.
In 1999, Southwest Airlines interviewed 90,000 people (out
of 140,000 applicants) to hire 4,200 employees. Obviously

the search for a new chief executive officer will not be that extreme, but the message is clear—conducting a thorough search is a time-consuming process.

All too often, the search process goes very smoothly and the finalists are great candidates, but then the interview process becomes rather shallow because the leaders of the search committee do not allocate adequate time for thorough analysis.

Appointment Agreement

This is an excellent device you can use to make sure everyone understands the scope of their commitment and the anticipated time that will be required of them. A typical appointment agreement lays out for each appointee the job description, including key dates, places of meetings, estimated length of meetings, deadlines, estimated duration of search, commitment to confidentiality, and so on.

An effective search committee is one where each member makes a valuable contribution to the process.

Seeing this in writing is helpful for search committee members. It gives them a dose of reality fairly early in the process. (For a sample, look in Appendix D.)

DETERMINING THE SIZE AND COMPOSITION OF THE SEARCH COMMITTEE

Finding balance on your search committee is easiest when the size of the committee has been determined ahead of time. There is no magic number for how many people should serve; I have seen effective groups as small as eight and as large as twenty-three, however my experience has shown that fewer than ten people makes the process work most smoothly.

Representational Strategy

Most search committees take a "representational" strategy when determining their compositions. That is to say, they

seek to have representation from the various constituents of their organization. For example, a committee searching to find the next president of a college or university would find it important to include: trustees, faculty, staff, alumni, and possibly students. And if the college or university has any religious affiliation, it is important to have someone active in that denomination represented as well.

When following the representational strategy, you'll inevitably have to include non-board members on your selection committee. You'll need to determine if these appointments will ultimately be decided by board members or by the key constituent groups? From our experience, the most effective way to appoint these search committee members is for each constituent group to nominate three to four people; the board or chairman of the board then picks appointees from among the nominees.

Younger-Board-Members Strategy

When working on a search for a social services agency in the Midwestern part of the United States, I quickly noticed that the composition of their board was divided. There was a small group of people whose tenure was in excess of twenty years. There was another group of directors who had only been on the board for five to seven years. For the most part, the group with five to seven years' experience were younger in age but had more years left to commit to the organization. For that reason, this group of six people was designated to be the search committee.

> The best searches are those whose committee members "trust the process."

A possible downside to this strategy is that by excluding the members with longer terms of service, you lose their perspective of the organization's history and traditions. Being aware of your organization's "sacred cows" can keep your search committee from making potentially drastic mistakes in its search process.

Past-Board-Chairs Strategy

One of the largest health and human services organizations in the United States uses the technique of having their CEO search committees made up of former board chairs. Part of the logic behind this decision is that you have knowledgeable individuals who have demonstrated commitment to the organization serving to select new leadership. These people are also aware of the history and traditions of the organization.

> Before agreeing to serve, make sure you can willingly give the time and attention required.

One benefit of having only volunteers, no paid staff, on the search committee is that employees are not put in a position of having to "choose sides." Instead, they have to trust the decision of the past board chairs to bring them the best candidate.

However, there are a couple of downsides to having only past chairmen serving on the search committee. One is the potential for a lack of diversity in gender or ethnicity. For instance, in the Deep South white males have traditionally chaired many not-for-profit boards. In this case, there is a need to go beyond past board chairs to achieve balance on the search committee. Another downside is that the local staff does not have ownership in the decision, and the transition of leadership may be a bit more difficult because of this.

Regardless of which of these strategies your board chooses, there is at least one other strategy to consider: assess the skills and natural talents the committee needs at this point in the life of the organization, and staff the search committee with constituents who bring these needed skills and natural talents.

CONSIDER NATURAL MOTIVATIONS OF THE SEARCH COMMITTEE MEMBERS

Each member of your search committee will view the search function through a unique lens. Imagine some of the following scenarios:

> What if the majority of the people on your search committee are so process oriented that it is difficult to make critical decisions?

> What if these process-oriented people are so analytical that the committee can't get past the details and analysis to let the process work?

> On the other hand, what if the majority of the members of your search committee are very bottom-line oriented. Are they accustomed to moving fairly quickly through the process to make the decision? As a rule, these types are easily frustrated by those who want to let the process work.

WHO SHOULD CHAIR THE SEARCH COMMITTEE?

In addition to finding balance and proper personality traits for each member of your search committee, it's important to choose the right person to lead this group. And as with other aspects of the process, arguments can be made for a variety of people to chair the search committee. Here are two scenarios:

Many times the Board will select one of their current or previous members to chair the search. In these cases the chairman of the board is an ex officio member of the search committee. If the chairman can restrain himself and let the appointed person actually lead the search, this can work well.

It is often the case that the chairman of the board will chair the search committee. The relationship between the board chair and the chief executive officer is key, which is why many search committees have this person direct their selection process. The more ownership the chairperson has in the decision, the better this relationship is likely to be. The main downside to this model is that leading the search committee doesn't give the chairman of the board much time to do the other important duties that are part of being an effective chairman.

QUALITIES OF EFFECTIVE SEARCH COMMITTEE MEMBERS

If you stop and think of the activities the search committee has to complete and the outcomes that you want from them, you can think of the natural motivations and qualities that the search committee chair needs to have an effective search. Here are the top characteristics you should require of any selection committee chairperson:

> He is someone to whom collaboration comes naturally.

> This person naturally takes the initiative and possesses the ability to draw people out of themselves and into action.

> He is slow to voice his opinion, but rather allows and encourages the group to talk thing through and come to their position.

> They enjoy combining their efforts and working jointly with others.

> They enjoy making others feel wanted and important as they get them to participate and contribute their talent and energy.

You can see that an effective search committee doesn't "just happen." It takes a lot of focused thinking and action to bring the right people together to conduct the search for your organization's next chief executive officer. By finding a balanced group of members with a variety of strengths and giftedness, and by choosing a chairperson with the appropriate level of drive and commitment, your committee will be well-positioned to find success in searching for your next executive leader.

Starting the Search

4

> Determining the search budget
> Assessing the health of your organization
> Opportunity Profile
> Critical Position Requirements
> Circumstances that influence the CPRs
> Critical Position Requirements interviews
> Getting the best input from your CPR interviews
> Documenting your findings and reaching consensus
> Understanding your candidate
> What is the board's charge to the search committee?

Now that you have prepared for the search and have selected your search committee, you are ready to actually begin your search! The next steps in the process of an executive search are some of the most crucial: assessing the health of the organization, writing the Opportunity Profile, and developing the Critical Position Requirements. As you will discover, spending adequate time in the development and writing of these documents can well determine the success of your search.

DETERMINING THE SEARCH BUDGET

The following line items should be considered when determining the search budget:

Travel Expenses—this includes travel expenses associated with bringing candidates to interview as well as travel

expenses of the search committee members. Will the search pick up committee member's travel expenses?

Off-Site Interview Facilities—it is often the case that the initial round of interviews will take place at an off-site location (i.e. retreat or conference center, large hotel such as a Marriott or Hilton, an airline club conference room at a major airport such as Delta's Crown Room, American's Admiral's Club, United's Red Carpet Club).

Costs associated with producing the Opportunity Profile—recently many organizations have began to use a web based Opportunity Profile. This is particularly attractive if the organization has in-house web design capability or can get this service donated. It is also gaining popularity because there are no printing costs associated with a web based model.

Communications related expenses—phone, postage, FedEx, etc.

Expenses associated with a search firm (if outside counsel is used)—this includes travel, lodging, meals, fees, postage, phone bill.

ASSESSING THE HEALTH OF YOUR ORGANIZATION

The dominant theme of the feedback I get from successful candidates for chief executive officer positions has to do with what they knew about the overall health of the organization before they assumed their leadership role. Most people wish that they had known more about this important aspect of the company they are getting ready to join. Although most search committees do not go to this length, there are several things that an organization can do to provide more meaningful information to their candidates.

Financial Audit

It can be helpful for potential candidates for a chief executive officer position to have a third party contextualize the financial health of the organization for them. This is more than the standard audit conducted by an accounting firm. Instead, it is an in-depth look at what's behind the numbers. Candidates who come from backgrounds in which they have not had significant profit-and-loss experience find this particularly helpful.

Board Audit

By the same token, it can be helpful both to the board and to the candidate to have a consultant who specializes in board development and leadership meet with the board and give them some feedback on the health of the board. This is particularly important if the board realizes that it has some areas of dysfunction that need addressing prior to bringing on a new CEO.

Morale Audit

The circumstances surrounding the need to conduct a search can have a significant impact on the morale of the employees of the organization, particularly if the overall health of the organization is not good. If the candidate gets to meet with enough people in the organization during the final interviews, she will get a sense of the nonprofit's morale, but some candidates have told me that it would have been helpful to know some specifics about the morale of the organization before they signed on for the job.

OPPORTUNITY PROFILE

Although it goes by various names, most search committees will develop a marketing piece to get the word out about the job opening. We call this an "Opportunity Profile." This is not a job description, but rather a marketing piece that discusses the organization and position in detail. So that the candidates can get a more comprehensive picture of the client organization, this document will usually direct anyone interested to the client's Web site address. If well written and

used correctly and effectively, the Opportunity Profile will get wide circulation.

I tell my clients that their Opportunity Profile is written to elicit one of two responses from the reader, either: "This job is for me. How do I apply?" or, "This job has Harry's name written all over it. He would be perfect for this job!" (And then they forward the Opportunity Profile to Harry, who would hopefully give the first response.)

A well-written Opportunity Profile can strengthen the pool of candidates, so getting it just right is important. There are different opinions on the best length for this document. On the surface it might appear that it should be concise and to the point, more like a comprehensive executive summary.

While there are certainly some potential candidates who prefer something more concise, our experience is that the Opportunity Profile should be comprehensive and complete. You are attempting to surface prospective candidates for the position; unless your organization has a high national profile and unaided name recognition, you need to take the time to properly introduce both your organization and the specific expectations for the chief executive officer position for the document to be useful.

The Opportunity Profile can be presented in various formats. Some of our clients continue to use a narrative document. Others prefer a graphic piece that resembles an annual report. Still others develop Web sites specific to the search. Whatever approach is taken, this document not only attracts potential candidates but helps build your brand with key constituents around the country.

CRITICAL POSITION REQUIREMENTS

Most people who are regularly involved in the identification and selection of senior executives agree that it is important to identify all the skills and abilities necessary to perform the job. Many people err on the side of generalizing what they believe to be the most critical executive skills and omitting often important but less obvious abilities needed.

A typical list of required skills would include:

leadership
the ability to motivate self and others
task oriented
creativity and insight
diplomacy and charisma
the ability to recruit a team
the ability to manage a team

In his article "Where Are the Leaders," which discusses leadership in not-for-profit organizations, Bob Carter writes that the characteristics that point to a successful nonprofit chief executive officer are:

Confidence: First, the individual must feel that he is capable of performing the job.

The charts on pages 31-32 are from a presentation by Nick Isbister (March 15, 2007). These are graphic representations of material from Robert Goffee and Gareth Jones, "Why Should Anyone Be Led by You?" Harvard Business Review. September/October 2000.

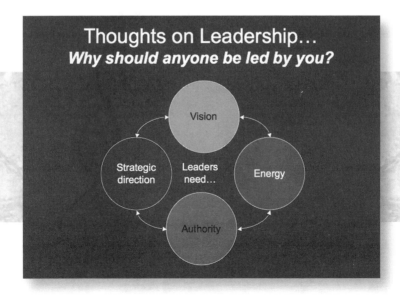

Humility: He must recognize that he will require help in non-familiar program areas—and must trust others to provide necessary guidance.

Risk Taking: A true leader takes risks by allowing for experimentation and events to occur without personal scrutiny.

Insight: He must demonstrate an understanding that the board governs and the CEO leads.

Vision: A CEO must create and articulate a vision to program and faculty personnel as well as the governing body.

Compassion: Without human touch and the recognition of the very humanity of relationships—specifically with those individuals expected to follow the leader and support the organization's goals—little time, motivation or inspiration will be found.

Responsibility: All leaders must possess the ability to say, "I was wrong," as well as "the buck stops here."

Judgment: A successful leader must recognize when to speak and when to listen.[3]

In his commentary in the January 23, 2004 issue of the *Wall Street Journal*, former GE Chairman Jack Welch discussed what he calls the Four Es of leadership:

> ❯ Successful leaders must have plenty of positive *energy*.

> ❯ They have to have the ability to *energize* others.

> ❯ They must have *edge*—the ability to make tough yes or no decisions.

> ❯ Finally, they must *execute*—get the job done.

In the same article, Welch went on to say that leaders also must have integrity, intelligence, and a passion for the job.

In general, it is difficult to argue with any of these elements. Surely you would expect most executives to have a reasonable share of these attributes. However, is this really all you need to know about what you are looking for in your next leader? Can you afford to be so general and vague about the specific skills and abilities that your next chief executive officer needs to have?

It Also Takes Courage to Lead

The point is not to become a leader. The point is to become yourself, and to use yourself completely—all your gifts, skills and energies—to make your vision manifest. You must withhold nothing. You must, in sum, become the person you started out to be, and to enjoy the process of becoming.

Warren Bennis, *On Becoming a Leader*

The main problem I have with these lists is that they are generated in the abstract and may not coincide with the specific leadership needs your organization has at this time in its history. To ensure that you hire the right chief executive officer, you must be sure that you know the specific needs of your organization.

Beware of the Pendulum Swing

Before getting any further into this topic, my co-author Nick has a great real-life client experience to share:

> Tom was in many respects a good chief executive officer for the organization. He certainly loved being able to promote the cause and speak at big conventions. He was always there on the podium at key events where the organization would want a presence. He had that "Clinton factor." When you met him he made you feel special. He made you feel important. He seemed to be interested in you. And his writing certainly helped keep the organization in the public eye. So in many respects he filled the bill as a great "public persona" for the organization.
>
> The fact that he wasn't really interested in running the show was a problem. All sorts of ill will festered in the organization; all sorts of issues were constantly brewing. The board even had a delegation from the staff at one point asking for everyone to address the problem of morale in the organization. The board liked the public profile the organization got and put some of the internal discontent down as a nasty and subversive form of jealousy.
>
> After a few years, Tom was recruited away by a larger and more prestigious organization. The board thought they would address the management issue squarely by going for a candidate with all the right management experience. They quickly decided that the best control

would come from an accountant. From flair (and even flamboyance) they moved to safety and control.

The accountant lasted less than a year. New donations to the organization took a nosedive. The truth was that the accountant was fair at conserving what was already there but dreadful at finding any new sources of income. He reinstituted great controls . . . but of diminishing resources and uninspired staff. The board's flip-flop approach didn't work!

The moral of this story is "don't rush into a critical hiring decision without taking a thorough look at the job and circumstances surrounding the change in leadership." The best way to determine what you are looking for in the next leader of your nonprofit is to develop what Nick and I call "Critical Position Requirements" or CPRs. Before you can determine if an individual is right for a particular job, you must know the specifics of that particular job. What will it really take to be successful in the position?

The CPRs of a job are those attributes, personal qualities, behaviors, and motivations that are required to do a specific job successfully. CPRs can be very helpful in the evaluation of candidates. Most of the people you choose to interview will be very professional and persuasive. They will probably have strong influencing abilities. However, in order to make a good hiring decision, you must keep in mind that while the chief executive officer probably needs strong influencing skills, the position is much more than having a good interview.

Note of Caution

All too often I find that my clients are tempted to confuse the CPRs with the job description or the Opportunity Profile. Remember, we are not talking about duties or responsibilities, but rather how a successful person actually does the job. For example, the job description for a running back would talk about receiving the handoff from the quarterback,

running away from would-be tacklers, reading blocks, running through gaps, and so on. However, the CPRs would talk about abilities such as rapid acceleration, sure grip on the ball, great field of vision, exceptional lateral agility, exceptional balance, ability to endure minor injuries and still perform, ability to absorb significant force from a hit or tackle and go right back to carrying the ball again on the next play.

CIRCUMSTANCES THAT INFLUENCE THE CPRS

There are a specific set of circumstances surrounding the changing of leadership in an organization. During a conference on CEO transitions that I attended, one of the women in the audience commented that every change in leadership she had observed was very circumstantial. Her observation was that it was dangerous to generalize when thinking about selecting a new leader for a nonprofit organization. She was a strong advocate for taking a serious look at the circumstances surrounding the change in leadership and basing the profile for the new leader on this analysis.

The Need for Change

Any time there is a vacancy at the top of a company or organization, there is the opportunity for change. A vacancy doesn't necessarily mandate change, but it does give the organization the opportunity to step back and evaluate the situation. In many ways, this is similar to what happens when a senior executive finds herself out of work. It is a good time for her to step back and take stock of where she has been, where she is, and where she wants to go in the future.

It is easy to talk about wanting change in the leadership of an organization, but it is often more difficult to actually hire someone who will bring the talked-about change to reality. I have worked with search committees who, in the early stages of the search, talked about making various levels of change in the style of their next leader. However, when it came time to study resumes and actually meet candidates, they were not as firm on the change as they had been in the beginning. This behavior manifests itself most often when members of the search committee begin to reminisce about the positive qualities of the outgoing chief executive officer.

In most cases, however, the consensus of the group rules with regard to the changes they want to see in their next leader, and they remember the discussions they had during the early phase of the search, when they agreed upon the direction of change they wanted. Nevertheless, there can be the temptation to leave things as status quo and hire someone very similar to the outgoing chief executive officer. My point here is to encourage the members of the search committee to remember the discussions and agreements they made in the early part of the search and stick to these commitments.

Do your homework with the candidates. If a change agent is what you want, be sure you know the strength of his experience in this area. If he is really a change agent, make sure you are ready for the changes he will bring. Talk with coworkers, trustees, and others from companies or organizations where he has worked in the past. Delve into the extent of the change he brought to those institutions and the positive and negative aspects of the change he brought. Above all else, ask yourself if the board is willing to stand behind the new chief executive officer when the troops rebel?

If your organization needs the level of change a "turnaround" requires, be aware that a true turn-around agent may need to move on to another turn-around situation before long. She won't be challenged by the status quo. What drives her is the desire to "fix" things, so she needs to have something that needs fixing in order to be able to apply her strengths and realize her deepest form of satisfaction. If nothing is broken, she just might find something to break in order to have something to fix. Consequently, a true turn around agent is rarely the person you want to hire for a long-haul position.

Current Health of the Organization

The current state of the organization has a lot to do with what you seek in your next chief executive officer. If the organization is on the brink of self-destruction, the CPRs will be quite different than if the organization were just coming off a ten-year period of growth and stability under a well-respected leader who is retiring on schedule. So you should evaluate your organization's current health—most easily done by surveying the leadership of the organization—before determining the CPRs for your new CEO. If the organization is not structurally sound, then the position will require someone who has a clear vision and can make necessary changes to return the organization to a state of health.

Conducting a survey at the beginning of the search. In some of our most successful searches, the search committee and other board leadership agreed that it was a good idea to do an organization-wide survey to collect information on how the employees viewed the health of the organization. This is the best time to hear from the employees regarding any changes they would like to see made or different directions in which they would like to see the new president take the organization.

In some instances, we will learn during the course of the survey process that the state of the organization is so unhealthy that the organization needs consultation in order to return to a healthy state before proceeding with their search. This situation can often occur if the organization doesn't have a well-defined organizational structure or a clear plan of succession, particularly if the current leader has a high profile and a great deal of name recognition, leaving "big shoes to fill" for his or her successor. Once the organization has a clear, as well as a sound organizational structure, it is then much easier to conduct a successful search for its next chief executive officer.

Using the Internet as a delivery system, it has become very easy to administer and tabulate the results of these organization-wide surveys. Given the employees of an organization can make an anonymous response via the Internet without fear of recrimination increases the likelihood that they will take the time to respond.

Expectations of the Board

Since the chief executive officer reports to the board, each board member should have ample opportunity to voice his or her opinions about the qualities needed in the next leader. This helps to achieve a diversity of perspectives that ensures all aspects of running your nonprofit are included in the criteria used to select your next CEO. For various reasons, board members will often view the changing of the chief executive officer as a time to consider bringing change to the organization as a whole.

Finances and Donor Relations

Most not-for-profit organizations depend upon contributions from a range of donors as the lifeblood of their existence. The state of this income stream will influence the kind of chief executive officer the organization should hire. It will also influence the level of administrative support the chief executive officer can expect, as well as the cost-conscious mindset the person has to have.

Place in the Organizational Life Cycle

Where an organization is in its corporate or organizational lifecycle has a lot to do with what you look for in your next leader. Many good journal articles and books have been written on this subject. One treatment of this reality that I like

---

Many of the ideas on pages 39-41 came from the following sources:

N. C. Churchill and V. L. Lewis, "Growing Concerns: The Five Stages of Small Firm Growth", Harvard Business Review. May/June 1983.

L. E. Greiner, Harvard Business Review. July/August 1972 and May 1998.

Adizes, Ichak, *Corporate Lifecycles: How and Why Corporations Grow and Die and What to do About It*, Prentice Hall 1988.

Gersick, Kelin E., et al., *Generation to Generation: Lifecycles of the Family Business*, Harvard Business School Press, 1997.

is the work of Ichak Adizes. He goes into great detail in his book *Corporate Lifecycles: How and Why Corporations Grow and Die and What to Do About It*. Although this was written about corporations in the private sector, I do believe that a lot of what he says is transferable to the not-for-profit sector.

Considering the ten stages of organizational growth that Adizes uses (Courtship, Infant, Go-Go, Adolescence, Prime, Stable, Aristocracy, Early Bureaucracy, Bureaucracy) one can easily think of the different leadership strengths and natural talents that it would take for someone to lead an organization in each of these stages of the lifecycle of an organization.

L. E. Greiner takes a different approach. He views growth as a series of changes forced by crises. Depending upon which stage the organization is in when new leadership is required will greatly impact the attributes and experience of the Chief Executive Officer you go after.

Adizes and Greiner's work tends to work best for large organizations. What if your not-for-profit is a small start up or small organization in general? N. C. Churchill and V. L. Lewis have developed a model that looks at small business.

Churchill and Lewis base their model on Greiner's and, like him, describe five stages: existence, survival, success, takeoff and, finally, resource maturity. This might be more suitable for a smaller not-for-profit. Their work has been published in the Harvard Business Review.

It is often the case that not-for-profit organizations are more like family held businesses than organizations that are more publicly held. *Generation to Generation: Life Cycles of the Family Business* (Harvard Business School Press) gives some perspective to this model.

I have to do a lot of organizational analysis in my work as a search consultant, particularly when I am working with a founder led organizations. However, I do not pretend to be an organizational development consultant. There are men and women in my organization who are specialists in this area and I utilize their expertise when needed. The point I want to make here is that the place that an organization finds itself when the need arises for new senior leadership will definitely impact the kind of person you seek at this time.

CRITICAL POSITION REQUIREMENTS INTERVIEWS

The Critical Position Requirements Interviews are a process that board members can use to enable them to determine what they want done in the job and, more importantly, how they want it done, thereby getting past any superficialities or generalities and down to the essential requirements by asking specific questions. I prefer to meet individually with all the people involved in the search—the board of directors, major donors, and the president's "cabinet" (all those who report to the president) and anyone in a senior leadership position who has a vested interest in the success of the new CEO.

As you summarize and synthesize what you hear in these interviews, you are looking for a pattern to emerge—one of behaviors and actions you want the next CEO to possess. For example, do you want someone with extraordinary vision,

who can "think outside the box," or do you need someone who can implement a vision already formulated? You are trying to draw a consensus from those whom you interview in this collaborative effort. In most cases, you will not be too far into the CPR interviews before you begin to notice a trend. However, occasionally the responses will seem scattered, and you will not observe a trend or pattern. In this case you have a problem; you have an organization in which the leadership does not have a clear vision for what they need in a new CEO.

Without clarity around the CPRs, you will have a very difficult time interviewing and evaluating candidates. If you find yourself in this confusing situation, read on! The following sections will tell you what you need to know to push forward through this complicated matter.

> **Without clarity around the CPRs, you will have a very difficult time interviewing and evaluating candidates.**

Who Should Participate in the CPR Interviews?

Many people within the organization and outside it will want to give their opinion on what skills or abilities the new CEO should possess, but there are certain individuals you should be sure to interview in-depth about their views. They are:

> **I have found that it is always best to spend time with each board member or trustee individually, as opposed to talking to the group as a whole.**

Those to whom the new hire will report. It is always a good idea for each board member to have the opportunity to confidentially express his or her views about what qualities and abilities the new executive needs to have. What are their expectations? After all, they are the ones the next chief executive officer ultimately has to please.

I have found that it is always best to spend time with each board member or trustee individually, as opposed to talking to the group as a whole. Group dynamics are powerful, and it is easy for the input of some to be diminished by the presence of others, particularly those who may have strong personalities.

Those who will report to the new hire. Although a new chief executive officer may choose to replace some of the current staff, a great deal can be learned about the organization from the people who report to this position.

Key donors. It is often a good idea to get input from significant individual donors, as well as the leaders of any foundations, large trusts, and so on, who are crucial to the financial success of the organization. These people have a vested interest in your nonprofit and will want to ensure that the organization remains successful. It is likely that they will have a good working knowledge of your organization as well; thus, their input can be invaluable.

What Questions Should You Ask?

Keep in mind that your objective is to determine both the current state of the organization and the behavioral qualities you are looking for in its next leader. Therefore, these interviews are best conducted by someone who is a good listener. He or she should know how to ask open-ended questions and how to avoid asking leading questions. Some of our preferred questions for getting to the heart of the issues the organization faces are in the sections below.

Questions about the individual you are interviewing.

> What is your role in the organization?
> How will you (or will you have) direct interaction with the person in this position?

Questions about the health of the organization, both structural and financial.

> How would you describe the current state of the organization?
> Where do you perceive the greatest problem areas to be?

> Have there been any ongoing problems?

> What are the three greatest challenges the new president will face?

> What particular challenges is the organization currently facing?

> What are the three greatest opportunities for the new Chief Executive to come in and make a reasonably quick impact?

Questions about the position itself.

> If the previous chief executive officer was not successful, discuss where he or she went wrong. Why was he not successful? Was it entirely his fault? Is the job a widow maker? Did the board have anything to do with his failure? Did he have an appropriate level of involvement and support from the board—not too much and not too little?

> If the previous chief executive officer was successful, discuss and elaborate on the things that he or she did right. (Note: You're aiming to learn from his best practices, not clone the prior CEO.)

> What education or experience does the person need in order to be effective in this job?

> What strengths does the person need to be effective in this job?

> What cautions do you have about the position at this time?

Questions about the internal politics at the organization.

> Are there conflicts within the chain of command?

> What are some landmines the next chief executive officer should be aware of?

> What are some opportunities the new chief executive officer will want to capitalize on?

You should end your interview by asking, "What advice or counsel can you give us about the search?" Some of the answers you uncover may surprise you; others may be consistent with the rest of the interviews you have conducted.

GETTING THE BEST INPUT FROM YOUR CPR INTERVIEWS

To get the best information during the critical requirements interviews keep the following in mind:

> Because you are looking for a pattern in the responses, ask each person roughly the same set of questions. Asking the same questions of each person interviewed gives validity to the pattern of responses.

> Don't accept vague generalities for responses; probe into what the person means. For example, if the interviewee says, "What we need around here is a leader," ask them to define "leader." What would a "leader" look like to them? Specifically, how would he or she lead? If someone says we want a "people person," find out what they mean by that. Some might define it as someone who is very outgoing and never met a stranger. Others might define a people person as someone who wants to please everyone. These are two very different meanings!

if the interviewee says, "What we need around here is a leader," ask them to define "leader." What would a "leader" look like to them? Specifically, how would he or she lead?

> Don't attempt to read between the lines or interpret what you are hearing. You will make your best observations when you simply record what you are hearing and summarize your findings.

DOCUMENT YOUR FINDINGS
AND REACH CONSENSUS

After you have completed the interviews, take time to summarize what you have heard and put these comments into eight to ten bullet points—these will become the document we call the "Critical Position Requirements." Circulate this among the board, and discuss your findings until the group reaches agreement on this document. Remember: this document contains the information against which you will be evaluating the finalists. It is, therefore, vitally important.

Keep the Critical Requirements to Yourself

As a search committee or board, it is very important that you keep the CPRs to yourself and not publicize them to the pool of candidates. In most cases, if candidates know what behaviors you are looking for, they will try to convince you that those behaviors characterize their leadership style. You are much better off when candidates come to the interview with the freedom to be themselves. You get a better picture of the person they will be once they settle into the job.

If your search committee does a good job of writing both the Opportunity Profile and the Critical Position Requirements, your search is much more likely to be successful. Writing both of these documents not only gives your search committee clarity in the type of person you are looking for, but it also gives you a guide to use in interviewing candidates and checking their references, both of which I will address later.

UNDERSTAND YOUR CANDIDATE

Search committees often make the mistake of allowing themselves to be enchanted by a long pedigree of qualifications or the person's charisma during the interview process. I ran into this once during a search for a new university president. During the early stages of the search, I discovered that one of the expectations of the new president was that she be visible on campus. This person was expected to have a high level of attendance and participation in campus activities: show up at athletic events, be there for musical productions, and so on.

Many of the board members were very highly impressed with one of the candidates. He had impeccable leadership experience. He was well published. His academic credentials were very strong. His connections with people of influence were as strong, if not stronger, than any of his peers'. He could have taken this university to new levels of endowment, achievement, and name recognition.

> One of my colleagues is fond of saying, "If you hold a gun to someone's head, they will do almost anything you ask them to do, but when you take the gun away, they will go back to what they naturally do and do best."

During the interview, however, he made it very clear that he saw his major contribution happening in meetings off campus and would conduct his presidency in this manner—he would not be highly visible on campus. While he understood that the students were a major part of the university environment, he was most effective with large donors and in meetings with high-ranking potential faculty members to discuss the possibility of their joining the university.

Our counsel to that board was that if they chose this man for their next president, they must accept the fact that he would conduct his presidency in this manner. Just because they asked him to have a high level of visibility on campus did not mean that he would do that. Because he knew that this was one of the expectations, he might be visible in the beginning, but as time passed and he began to settle into his routine, he would go back to his natural way of operating.

One of my colleagues is fond of saying, "If you hold a gun to someone's head, they will do almost anything you ask them to do, but when you take the gun away, they will go back to what they naturally do and do best." Another puts it this way: in selecting a leader we want to know more about his "want-tos" than his "can-dos" or "will-dos." His logic is

that all of us *can* do a lot of things, but when left to choose, we will do what we *want* to do.

Both research and our many years of experience indicate that this is a fact, no matter how distasteful it may be to the conventional thinking of most Americans, which is summed up in the old adage, "You can do anything you put your mind to." This may be true—but only for a little while. As I have addressed earlier in the book, you have a recurring pattern of motivations—both genetic and learned—that is far more powerful and enduring than any short-term "pep talk" you may give yourself about "unlimited potential." In many cases, you do have "unlimited potential," but it is within the scope of the abilities and driving motivators that create your unique set of abilities—the crossroads of what you can do well (ability) and what you want to do, or those things that give you tremendous satisfaction in doing them (motivation). Defining your Critical Position Requirements early in the search process and sticking to this list when interviewing potential candidates for the job will enable you to avoid making the mistake of ignoring the truth about his or her personality or temperament and will give you the ability to make a wise decision in hiring your next chief executive officer.

> **Define your Critical Position Requirements early in the search process and sticking to this list when interviewing potential candidates.**

WHAT IS THE BOARD'S CHARGE TO THE SEARCH COMMITTEE?

One of the questions I ask at my initial meeting with the search committee is "What is the Board's charge to the search committee? Have they commissioned you to bring them one candidate or are you to bring them the top two or three candidates?" This may not seem significant, but it is.

By the time the search committee gets to the short list of candidates, you will have a lot of hours invested in learning about these candidates. You will have interviewed them a couple of times. You probably spent time on the phone with them prior to the interviews. You have checked their references. In short, you know a lot about these people and you know why you elevated them to the short list above all of the other men and women in the pool.

The Board is placing a lot of trust in the work and judgment of the search committee if they charge you to bring them your top candidate. I don't want to imply that the Board will "rubber stamp" your nominee, but it is a fact that when they interview this person, they will not learn nearly as much as you have learned. My experience is that as a group, they will spend at most a couple of hours with the candidate. They are placing a lot of responsibility on the search committee to know what is best for the organization and to find the best person for the job.

The Board is trusting that you will spend adequate time in the search process to identify the best person.

If they charge you with bringing them the top two or three candidates, they will need to spend adequate time with these candidates. Whether they can learn as much as you have learned is highly doubtful.

Here is where trust enters into the picture. If they charge you to bring them one candidate, they are placing a lot of trust in you. They are trusting that you will spend adequate time in the search process to identify the best person. If they charge you to bring them two or three candidates, they need to trust that you have brought them the best of the pool. Their role should be to decide which of these should be the next president. They do not have the time, nor should they take the time, to "start from scratch" with these candidates. They have to trust that they are starting with two or three highly qualified candidates and go from there.

It is a much cleaner process if the charge from the board is to bring the top candidate.

What should you do? That is not my decision; it has to be made by the board or the Executive Committee of the Board. When asked, my counsel to boards is that it is a much cleaner process if the charge from the board is to bring the top candidate.

Sourcing: The Meat of the Search

5

HIGHLIGHTS

> Sourcing

> Sourcing through networks

> Using the Opportunity Profile

> Time needed for sourcing

> Advertising

Once you have written the Opportunity Profile and Critical Position Requirements for your next CEO, your search committee has a clear understanding of exactly what you are looking for in your next leader. You are now ready to begin the meat of the search, which I call sourcing.

Sourcing is the process you use to get the word out about your search to various strategic networks. In this chapter I will discuss the use of advertising as well. Both sourcing and advertising are methods you can use to publicize your search and discover potential candidates.

SOURCING

Sourcing is a crucial phase of the search process. This is when word goes out that you are conducting a search. Your goal is to attract a large pool of qualified potential candidates. Thorough sourcing assures that you will surface individuals beyond the pool of usual or suspected applicants. It takes time

to penetrate new networks; in fact, the sourcing process is probably the most time-consuming part of the search because it involves meeting with, calling, or emailing all of your contacts to let them know you are looking for a new CEO.

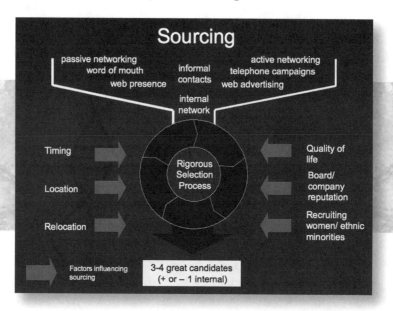

It is helpful to view the sourcing phase of the search as a funnel. The top of the funnel is the place where the sourcing begins. Early in the sourcing process you are casting a very broad net to all possible candidates. These names come to you through any number of avenues: through word of mouth, various formal and informal networks, professional associations, and so on. Usually the best candidates come via an aggressive outbound telephone campaign, in which a designated person makes a serious effort to contact either potential candidates or people who can lead you to potential candidates.

SOURCING THROUGH NETWORKS

Sourcing through networks is an extremely helpful aspect of your search. As your committee members each go about notifying their networks about your particular leadership needs, they will be tapping into other established networks. Thorough sourcing brings candidates into the pool who might otherwise not have considered the position, and it surfaces names of people from the private sector who have been considering making a career move to the not-for-profit sector.

Generally speaking, candidates that come through sourcing in networks are those people who have the skills and experience you need for the particular position. One reason for this is that the point person who is handling the telephone interaction with this large network is taking the time to tell people about the position and the kind of experience your organization wants their next leader to possess. Additionally, the point person is getting a copy of the Opportunity Profile in the hands of these contacts, many times going through the hands of several layers of people, before ending up with someone who recognizes the opportunity it could provide for him and his career.

Another reason sourcing produces such qualified candidates is that the point-person who is handling the telephone interaction typically has some level of relationship with the person with whom she is talking. As a rule, those making recommendations recognize that their reputations are on the line when they suggest someone who is not going to be a good fit for the position.

A Note of Caution

A note of caution should be exercised here. The fact that a name comes to you through someone's network does not necessarily mean that the individual is qualified to provide leadership to your organization.

All of us have well-meaning friends and business associates who will pass along the names of their friends without really learning enough about the job to know if the suggested person would be a good fit. In some cases it can get politically

"sticky," when it comes to rejecting these people as potential candidates.

USING THE OPPORTUNITY PROFILE

At the early stage of sourcing, your primary concern is to attract a sufficiently large pool of candidates from as broad a base as possible. This is where the use of the Opportunity Profile comes in. You will need to email or send hard copies of this document to your entire network of contacts. In many cases I will condense the Opportunity Profile into a one-page version of highlights, called the Executive Summary. This document gives a shorter history of the organization, a briefer explanation of your nonprofit's organizational structure, and a short summary of the job description of the CEO position. In the Executive Summary, I will refer the reader to the Opportunity Profile posted on our Web site, as well as to the Web site of the organization. I have found that most contacts prefer reading a shorter version initially, and then, if they are interested in more information, they can go to the full-length Opportunity Profile online. Mailing or E-mailing the Executive Summary rather than the entire Opportunity Profile is more cost efficient as well.

Your goal at this point is to cast a wide net and get the information about this opportunity into as many networks as possible. When you send out your Executive Summary, you will want to ask each of your contacts to forward it to anyone within their network of contacts whom they think might be both interested and qualified. This greatly broadens the net that you have cast. Once you have sent out the Executive Summary, you should follow up with the contacts you think will be most interested or who might know the most qualified, interested candidates. You can then send them a copy of the full Opportunity Profile if they would like more information. Additionally, you must follow up with anyone referred to you by your initial contacts.

TIME NEEDED FOR SOURCING

It's always one of the questions asked early in the search: some variation of "how long is this going to take?" That's always a tough question because we really don't know how long it is going to take to surface a sufficient number of qualified candidates. In most cases, the usual group of unqualified, marginally qualified and those who are out of work will appear in the first week or two. Occasionally, you will find one or more finalists in this group, but the best candidates usually come after persistent research. Eventually, you will "smoke them out."

This is indeed a time-consuming process, but if done properly, thorough sourcing can greatly strengthen your pool of candidates. Oftentimes nonprofits don't have the time it takes to do the sourcing process as thoroughly as they should, but it is crucial and will have a direct effect on the outcome of your search. This is not an area that you want to short-circuit.

Many people on search committees say that their preference for the next chief executive officer is someone who has been very successful at a similar organization and who will do an as-good or better job for them as he has done for his current employer. This is not an easy find! Even if you introduce your opportunity properly, it will generally take some persistent persuading to lure this person to your organization.

As more people from the private sector continue to evaluate opportunities for service in the not-for-profit sector, search committees will have the opportunity to talk with candidates who have been very successful in the business world. If you are interested in these people, you must be prepared to take the time to thoroughly introduce them to your organization. This is a big decision for them, and it will take some time for the individual and his or her family to reach a decision. Not everyone from the private sector can make the shift successfully. It is better to know this earlier than later. Give these people time to discover if the job fits.

> If you truly want to give the market the opportunity to provide you with a pool of high-quality candidates, you have to give the sourcing process time to work.

If you truly want to give the market the opportunity to provide you with a pool of high-quality candidates, you have to give the sourcing process time to work. Later you will evaluate the candidates who have surfaced against your criteria: the Critical Position Requirements.

Placing Time Limits on the Search

There are times when the circumstances around the search require that you have a deadline for considering applications. For me this happens most frequently in academic searches where many of the candidates operate on an annual contract and the timing of the appointment of the new president needs to coincide with the academic calendar.

ADVERTISING

Once I heard someone attribute the following quote to world-renowned management consultant, Peter Drucker: "The problem with advertising is that half of it doesn't work. The trick is to determine which half."

While working on a search for a college president, we were discussing whether to advertise anywhere other than *The Chronicle of Higher Education*. I shared this quote with the search committee, and one of the trustees said that he was sure that at least half of their advertising didn't work. In fact, he said his experience was that 80 percent didn't work.

As you talk with individuals who have previously served on search committees, you will most likely get a wide range of comments about the effectiveness of advertising. The advantage of advertising is that depending on where you advertise, you can potentially get a very broad range of coverage and exposure. You can also, however, spend a small fortune on advertising. In light of this, I have learned that the best use of advertising dollars is to communicate enough about your job opening to convince someone to visit a Web site where a more comprehensive overview of the job is posted.

I had my first experience with this when I was conducting the search for the president of one of the world's largest NGOs (non-government organizations). The board of directors wanted to run an ad in the *Wall Street Journal*. One of the directors had been successful in recruiting a chief financial officer for her organization through advertising in the *Journal,* and she thought this would be a good way to attract some potential candidates.

In this case, the client placed a well-worded advertisement that hooked people into visiting their Web site to learn more about the job. When you got to their Web site, there was a link to a very comprehensive overview of the organization and the position.

By advertising in this manner, the client was the winner in two ways. First, they got people, who otherwise may have never heard of their organization, to visit their Web site. Additionally, we did get a couple of good potential candidates from this advertisement.

Note of Caution

If you decide to advertise in a major periodical and you are using a search firm, check the difference between what the periodical will charge the firm to place the ad and their rates for not-for-profit organizations. For some periodicals the rates are significantly higher, for for-profit companies than they are for nonprofits.

Possible Downsides to Advertising

One of the downsides to advertising is that you are going to hear from countless people who are in no way qualified to lead your organization. Someone has to examine these resumes to weed through the useless ones. And if you choose to respond to every inquiry, this will be a very time-consuming task for someone in your organization. The temptation is to delegate

this to a clerk or some lower-paid person who can get the job done with a minimum of expense. The trouble with this is that a person at that skill level is not likely to be as familiar with the position or with the variety of experiences and backgrounds of the candidates. It is best to have someone who knows the organization and position do this.

A second downside to advertising if your not-for-profit organization has a strong set of core values, is that not everyone who responds to your announcement may share these values. You may receive resumes that look very strong from a functional perspective. What you don't know, however, is how well this person lines up with your organization. And because the words and actions of the leadership of your nonprofit need to be consistent with the values the organization claims to uphold, you may waste valuable time conducting in-depth interviews only to discover that your values are not coherent.

> **The most effective way to find exceptionally qualified candidates is through the painstaking effort of sourcing through networks.**

In summary, while there is some inherent value in advertising your CEO position, I have found over the years that the most effective way to find exceptionally qualified candidates is through the painstaking effort of sourcing through networks.

Factors that Influence the Quality of the Pool

6

> **Timing**
> **Location**
> **Quality of work and leisure issues**
> **Your organization's reputation on the street**
> **Viewing candidates as "damaged goods"**
> **Recruiting women and ethnic minorities**

Somewhere in the process of sourcing, a committee member will ask: "Do we have the best possible candidate we could get for this position?" There are many factors that influence who will become a serious candidate for a specific position. Any combination of these can impact the pool of finalists for any given search.

TIMING

Timing is everything in the search process. Often candidates will tell me that they are very interested in working for my client, but the timing of the search doesn't work with their current situation. Many different timing issues can influence your search, such as:

The candidate's children and their status in school. If a couple has a child who is a junior in high school, often they are reluctant to relocate until the child has graduated.

Timing is everything in the search process.

Aging parents or family health issues. We seem to be living in a time in which people are more sensitive to family commitments. I have had candidates who were very interested in jobs but declined the position because of the ages or health of their parents.

Stress of relocation and other family issues. Occasionally a candidate will tell me that his family has recently undergone some level of stress, and it just wouldn't be right to add that the stress of relocating his family at this time.

LOCATION

There is an adage in real estate that says that the three most important things are location, location, location. The location of a job cannot be overlooked as a corporation or organization thinks about filling positions.

If it is not clear in the Opportunity Profile, it is common for candidates to ask me very early in the conversation about the location of the job. There are many nuances involved in this question. For some people, location has to do with the quality of schools for their children. For others, it's the size of the community in which they will live. There are some very good not-for-profit organizations headquartered in semi-rural areas. Some people do not care to live or raise their family in a small to mid-sized town, but there are many who would see this as an advantage, with lower crime rates, stronger sense of community, and so on.

The fact is that most organizations are not going to relocate their headquarters, so you must make the most of your situation and package the position so that those who would be attracted will learn about the opening.

Relocation

Some employers today are meeting resistance when it comes to asking Generation Xers (anyone born between 1965 and 1980) to uproot their families and move them numerous times. This is also true for Gen Xers considering internal promotions with their current employer.

I serve on an informal advisory board of a large national social services agency. This organization has a preference to promote from within rather than go outside the organization for new leaders. One afternoon I received a call from one of the board members. I could tell from the tone of her voice that she was very frustrated. She shared with me that after spending two days with an internal candidate from one of the organizations offices in another city, the employee finally told them that she couldn't accept the position because it required relocation and she didn't want to leave her hometown. The board member went on to say that this wasn't the first time this had happened to them. Nationally this agency was having a hard time getting people from Generation X to make geographic moves to advance their careers. My observation of culture is that Xers as a group want it all; delayed gratification is not high on their list of values.

In an effort to make moving more palatable to your potential candidates, be sure that your relocation package is a generous one—one that allows not only for general moving and relocation expenses but also for one or more house-hunting trips. You might also need to consider reimbursement of rental expenses while your new hire is trying to settle into his or her new location. Many CEOs prefer to live in the community awhile before deciding which area of town is the best location for them. Candidates moving from the private sector to the nonprofit sector may be prepared to take salary cuts, but they want to make sure that their families are sufficiently provided for and that the stress of relocation is kept to a minimum. Offering good relocation benefits helps to ensure that the transition will be a smooth one.

YOUR ORGANIZATION'S REPUTATION ON THE STREET

Every now and then it is good for an organization to get a reality check on how they are perceived by the public. Sometimes

there are things going on in an organization that the leadership either is blind to or refuses to believe. If these things continue, they will impact the reputation of the organization. Whether done formally or informally, the results of this analysis should be taken seriously.

Some areas of possible concern potential candidates might have are:

> Does your organization have a good reputation and policy of promoting from within?

> Does your organization encourage or allow its employees to place family as a high priority in their lives?

> What is the rate of turnover in your organization?

> What happened to the previous holder of the position for which you are considering me?

> What is the financial stability of your organization?

In order to attract top candidates, these issues need to be considered and addressed. As I have mentioned, attracting quality candidates to the search process can be difficult. I have worked on searches in which some of the people we desired for the position chose not to participate in the process. In some cases, they had heard things about the board that didn't appeal to them.

Board Reputation

What kind of reputation does your board have? Questions about the board never fail to come up as a candidate begins to move toward the short list. Some of the questions that are often asked are:

> Tell me about the board. Are they micromanagers?

> I've heard that some of the board members got in the way of the last CEO. What do you know about that?

> Is the board a fund-raising board or a figurehead board?

> Is the board going to allow the next CEO to do his or her job?

> What does the board believe about governance? Does their walk match your talk?

I never cease to be amazed at how the news about not-for-profit boards travels. If an organization has any degree of high profile, the reputation of the board will be known to a large number of people.

What kind of reputation does your board have?

VIEWING CANDIDATES AS "DAMAGED GOODS"

In some instances I have seen candidates who would participate only if, in their minds, they had a very good chance of being selected. Many of these were reluctant to enter the process because they had been in other searches in which they made the short list, only to be the "bridesmaid." People who think like this have a fear that being the "bridesmaid" too many times could damage their careers, to which there is an element of truth.

I have worked on searches in which, during the sourcing phase, I would meet with the search committee to hold initial discussions regarding people whose names had been suggested. Occasionally I have mentioned a name, only to have one of the members say something like, "You know, she was a finalist in the XYZ search. I thought she was a very strong candidate, and yet she wasn't selected. The search committee there must have discovered something they didn't like. We don't want anything to do with her."

I remember a specific instance in which we were moving toward determining the makeup of the short list. One person's name continued to be mentioned favorably. As I was giving the committee a summary of this man's experience,

his qualifications, and the information that I was hearing as I discussed his potential candidacy with sources from within my network, I casually mentioned that he had recently been involved in a similar search with another well-known non-profit. He had made it to a short list of two, only to lose out to the other candidate. Immediately, some of the members of the committee started looking at this person as "damaged goods." I had a very difficult time getting them to take a serious look at him. In the end we eliminated his name from discussion.

I thought that this was a serious mistake, because he was an excellent candidate. His track record was very strong. I knew members of that search committee, as well as the firm that was conducting the search for the other organization. His not being chosen for that position had very little to do with his qualifications. In the end, that organization made their decision strictly on the personality of the other candidate. It seemed unfair that this man was perceived as "damaged goods." As often as this happens, it is easy to see why some very good candidates are sometimes reluctant to "throw their hats into the ring."

RECRUITING WOMEN AND ETHNIC MINORITIES

If your organization is interested in attracting women or ethnic minorities to positions of senior leadership, board members need to be prepared for serious candidates to want to know what percentage of leadership within your organization is held by minorities. If they are going to be pioneers in your organization, they are likely to approach the search process with a healthy skepticism.

Another issue that minority candidates might have is that of being a "token" interviewee. I have been told on many occasions, "I already have plenty of good experience in interviewing. I get telephone calls from people like you every week. I don't have time to interview just to please someone's desire to have an African-American in the pool of candidates." It is both unfair to them and to the other candidates to include any minority contenders merely because you want to add diversity to your pool of candidates.

Finally, the composition of your search committee can have an impact on how successful you are in attracting people of different ethnicities to your pool. If your search committee is composed of all white males (or all white females), and you want to attract a diverse pool of candidates, that sends a negative message to prospective candidates.

While some of these factors are outside your control—such as the location of the organization or relocation requirements for the position—others can be managed and even improved by your board. You need to consider them and be able to present them to your pool of candidates in a positive light.

It Also Takes Courage to Lead

The point is not to become a leader. The point is to become yourself, and to use yourself completely—all your gifts, skills and energies—to make your vision manifest. You must withhold nothing. You must, in sum, become the person you started out to be, and to enjoy the process of becoming.

Warren Bennis, *On Becoming a Leader*

Identifying Your Candidate's Motivated Abilities

7

> Understanding natural or "innate" strengths

> Identifying the Motivated Abilities Pattern© or MAP

> The MAP: a system of behavior

> Applying the MAP to the search committee selection process

One of the first courses I took in my doctoral program was Research Methodology. On the first day of class the professor asked us to write a paper about our personal biases. It was his conviction that everyone brings certain biases to everything they do, including research and writing, and it is best to acknowledge these biases from the outset.

Early in the writing of this book, I realized that I bring a set of biases to the search process. In fairness to you, the reader, I believe it is best to let you know some of these biases. My basic belief about the nature of people strongly influences my observations about them, and thus the counsel I provide in the hiring process.

UNDERSTANDING NATURAL OR "INNATE" STRENGTHS

This is the golden nugget of human nature: Each person has an innate ability and motivation to achieve a certain unique purpose, and through that purpose to find rich personal

satisfaction and make a distinct contribution to society. Our equality does not lie in the nature of our talents but in the fact that we each are endowed with our own unique purpose.

People are born with a unique *modus operandi*, a defined way of functioning, a pattern of certain competencies and motivations that governs how they attempt to perform any job or role. I refer to innate motivation as a person's *giftedness* or *natural strengths* because it is an endowment or inheritance, if you will, as contrasted to the results of a developmental process.

> **People are born with a unique *modus operandi*, a defined way of functioning, a pattern of certain competencies and motivations that governs how they attempt to perform any job or role.**

Giftedness is an observable and provable fact of human nature. Evidence for this innate and unique make-up goes back as far as Socrates ("know thyself and become who you are") and is as current as the expressions of Jung, Adler, Fromm, May, Goldstein, Rogers, Allport, Maslow, and Drucker. But, oddly enough, the concept of *giftedness* has been ignored throughout most of this century by mainstream thought in business and management.

Many managers still believe in their powers to "mold and shape" employees to become what they need. They continue to make critical decisions about hiring, promoting and transferring people primarily on the basis of the individual's past performance as observed, evaluated and reported by others (e.g., college degrees, grade point average, references, 360 degree feedback, performance appraisals). The resulting decisions are effectively a crapshoot. At least 50 percent of the time, people who are not good at (or motivated to) make risky decisions, set new and different goals, or monitor activities which impact on bottom-line issues are promoted into key positions that require these specific "motivated" abilities. The impact of this pervasive mismatch on productivity, growth, efficiency, costs, and workforce morale is practically beyond

> **The concept of *giftedness* has been ignored throughout most of this century by mainstream thought in business and management.**

measure. Why? Because each mismatch not only affects productivity of the incumbent, but also creates impediments in the performance of all those up, down, and sideways who interact with and rely on the mismatched person.

IDENTIFYING THE MOTIVATED ABILITIES PATTERN (MAP)©

Giftedness emerges in people's lives as a consistent pattern of behavior whenever they do something they feel they have done well *and* they have enjoyed doing. Once you understand a person's giftedness, you understand the kind of work assignment that will engage his heart and mind. You know what he will and will not deliver. You know what she will avoid, and where she will get into trouble. Because giftedness is irrepressible and constantly seeking expression, it is manifested throughout people's lives every time they do something they find satisfying and believe they do well.

> **Giftedness emerges in people's lives as a consistent pattern of behavior whenever they do something they feel they have done well *and* they have enjoyed doing.**

The authority for these observations comes from more than forty-five years of studying the lived achievement experiences of more than eighty-five thousand people— the People Management International, LLC, clients from all over the world. Beginning in the early 1960s, Arthur Miller and Ralph Mattson developed a process called the System for Identifying Motivated Abilities (SIMA)©. Their methodology provides both the language and the process for identifying innate giftedness. The resulting description of a person's giftedness based on recurring behavioral evidence is called the Motivated Abilities Pattern©. To more fully appreciate the phenomena of giftedness patterns, you must first learn more about the evidence for these patterns and how to utilize that evidence to identify recurring themes.

While a person may be aware of some aspects of her recurring motivations, she usually does not recognize the complete pattern until it is fully described. Most people have simply

not been made aware of the existence of these patterns, nor have they had the opportunity to identify their own patterns. In my experience, the most effective way to learn about these patterns is to work with examples or case studies. Let's start with Shane, a researcher at a biomedical laboratory. Shane has prepared the following descriptions of achievements from his work and life that meet the two criteria for the MAP analysis: that Shane (1) enjoyed doing them and (2) felt he did them well. As you read these achievements, make some notes of the recurring themes you recognize in Shane's data.

Shane's Achievement Data

Collecting

Read about everything I could get my hands on, interested in invertebrates . . . always looking for different types of worms, etc. Fascinated to see particular organisms . . . always looking for new types . . . fascinated with finding unusual types. Did experiments, made cuts in worm, grew two heads, two tails.

Research Project—School

Conducted an extensive research project for a class . . . extensive research project . . . Physiological Changes in Limpets in Response to Escape Eliciting Substances. Worked on project two months beyond course despite lack of cooperation from professors. Very interesting . . . fascinating complex of behaviors. Figured out some kind of experiment . . . animals showed very interesting responses. Some were quite absurd . . . nobody really looked at the physiology of this thing. Fascinated by the whole subject . . . presence of the extract resulted in increase in heart rate and respiration.

Research Project—Work

Discovered two mechanisms involved in response to simulated jet lag in monkeys. Discovered during analysis of data . . . looked for something that was cohesive. Discovered different pattern in data of one monkey. Pursued it to point where I got this presentation . . . took data and explained . . . fascinating in that I had discovered this and didn't expect to see it—really interesting.

Identifying the MAP includes examining the achievement data (both written and oral) for "evidence" in the actual words that the achiever used to describe what he remembered about the selected experiences. For example, in examining Shane's achievement data, the following evidence and related themes can be observed:

Evidence	Theme
read, interested in, looking for	Investigating
did experiments, made cuts, figure out	Analyzing
really look at, discovered	Observing
some kind of experiment, made cuts in worms	Experimenting
invertebrates, worms, organisms	Physiology
physiological, limpets, animals fascinated to see, looking for new types, excited to find, discovered two mechanisms, discovered different patterns, fascinating that I had discovered this, didn't expect to see this	Discovery

THE MAP: A SYSTEM OF BEHAVIOR

The analysis of thousands of MAPs has revealed five distinct aspects of motivation that are present in the achiever's description of his or her activities. These five aspects of motivation are interdependent, thus it is important to think of the pattern as a *system of behavior, each part enabling as well as restraining the other parts.* The five aspects are listed and described below, and examples of each are provided. They are also used to create a framework for the evidence identified in Shane's achievement data.

Motivated Abilities

Some of your abilities are *motivated*, which means you never get bored or tired of using them. You use these abilities repeatedly in activities you find rewarding and enjoyable. Most of us have a long list of abilities we can perform, but "motivated" abilities are the ones that continually recur in the achievements we enjoy doing and feel we do well.

Shane's motivated abilities include investigating, analyzing, observing, and experimenting. Others may be motivated by influencing, communicating, overseeing, creating, organizing.

Subject Matter

This is what a person is interested in or what a person is motivated to work with or through. It may range from something very concrete, such as "animals" or "vehicles," to something that is intangible such as values, ideas, theories, etc.

Shane's subject matter is very focused; he is primarily interested in living organisms. Many people have three to

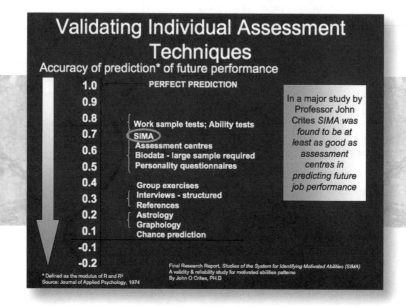

five areas of "motivated" subject matter (e.g. numbers, people, concepts, structures, methods, tools, or devices).

Circumstances

There are certain factors that trigger your motivation and certain environments that transform you into a highly motivated person. For example, some people need clear objectives in order to function. Others develop direction as they go. Some people function best under stress, in emergencies, or in situations that would render another immobile.

Shane is motivated by circumstances that provide him freedom to experiment. Others may be motivated by competition, projects, causes, results, profit, recognition, or a host of other circumstances.

Operating Relationship

There is a particular way in which you prefer to relate to others in a work situation. Your operating relationship has nothing to do with whether you are sociable or not, or whether you are introverted or extroverted. Your operating relationship only describes your preferred relationship to others when you are performing activities that are most satisfying and rewarding for you.

Individual contributors want to occupy a well-defined role and to be able to secure results through their own efforts. People who are motivated to accomplish their work as individualists may at times involve others in their work, but they are not a good "fit" for jobs that require them to have overall responsibility for the work of others. (Note: This is simply a "fit" issue, and not a deficiency in the candidate. In fact, the majority of highly rated knowledge workers who command "expert" status roles are motivated to work as individualists. In a team environment, they are most productive when given a specific assignment that is later integrated into the work of the team. While this may sound contrary to the current

training on "teamwork," effective supervisors know this is
how it really works best.)

Key contributors gravitate toward roles, positions, and
involvements that are *crucial* to the success of an operation,
project, or program or to the *needs and goals* of people. They
want a specific application in making the whole effort successful. Like the individual contributor, they tend to function
as a distinctive contributor, rather than merge their effort
with others.

Team members want to sense that people are dependent
and supportive of one another and act out of a sense of commitment to the team goals and purposes.

People are motivated to relate to others in a variety of ways
when achieving their purposes, including as a team member,
spearhead, trainer, enabler, coach, facilitator, director, man-
ager, or leader. A person may be motivated to perform in more
than one of these operating relationship roles, but only about
25 percent of the population is truly motivated to seek overall
responsibility for outcomes and to oversee the work of others.
This means that while there are many people who want to be
managers or leaders, it does take some skilled investigation to
identify those who possess the innate *giftedness* for the job.

An analysis of Shane's achievement stories indicates that
Shane is motivated to work as an individual contributor. He
functions in an individualistic way. His achievement stories
reveal that he has an inclination toward solitary and independent activity where his work reflects his own style and effort.

Motivational Payoff

At the core of your motivation is a singular, uniquely char-
acteristic outcome that you seek in order to feel a sense of
accomplishment and satisfaction. This payoff is *not* simply a
pleasure-seeking outcome; it is the fulfillment that comes with
performing activities that achieve your particular purpose.
The payoff can be achieved from any kind of activity, those

with your family, in school, in a job, playing a sport, in a religious organization, or through volunteer work. The joy and fulfillment that comes with achieving your payoff keeps you "coming back for more" throughout your entire life.

The outcome or payoff that Shane seeks is the discovery of something new. He is also motivated when he is involved in the discovery process.

In contrast, some people are motivated when they are able to excel, gain recognition, or in some way differentiate their performance from others. Yet others want to exert dominance and willpower, be in charge, or overcome obstacles. Many people feel particularly fulfilled and satisfied when they meet a goal, need, or challenge. Others want to effect a change on a person, object, or situation, as in gaining a response or making an impression. Usually, only one of these payoffs dominates an individual's achievement data. Other payoffs may be present but are more likely to be the means to the end, not the end in itself. It is this end point, or the Motivational Payoff, that individuals are least likely to recognize and understand.

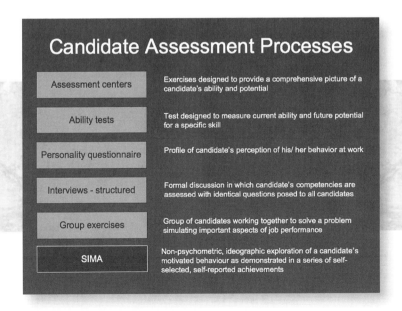

Candidate Assessment Processes

Assessment centers	Exercises designed to provide a comprehensive picture of a candidate's ability and potential
Ability tests	Test designed to measure current ability and future potential for a specific skill
Personality questionnaire	Profile of candidate's perception of his/ her behavior at work
Interviews - structured	Formal discussion in which candidate's competencies are assessed with identical questions posed to all candidates
Group exercises	Group of candidates working together to solve a problem simulating important aspects of job performance
SIMA	Non-psychometric, ideographic exploration of a candidate's motivated behaviour as demonstrated in a series of self-selected, self-reported achievements

APPLYING THE MAP TO
THE SEARCH COMMITTEE SELECTION PROCESS

Let us apply what we have learned about giftedness to the task of selecting appropriate members for the search committee.

The following is a nomination for Dr. John Doe to serve as the chairperson for the search committee that is selecting the Director of the Happy Valley Parks and Recreation Board. This board governs a powerful service group, located in a rural area that is experiencing rapid population growth.

> To Whom It May Concern:
>
> For the position of chairperson, I respectfully submit the name of Dr. John Doe. John has lived in the community for several years since his retirement. During his career as a scientist, he was renowned for his discoveries and patents. His publications have appeared in many referred journals. His PhD from UC-Berkeley was awarded with distinction, and he has been designated a fellow by the American Academy of Sciences.
>
> Since moving to our community, John has been an active member of the People's Church. Dr. Doe has indicated that his retirement leaves him with plenty of time to fulfill the responsibilities the chair of this search committee would require.
>
> Submitted by Pastor Tom Jones
> Member, Happy Valley Parks
> and Recreation Board

Dr. John Doe does have an impressive set of credentials and is no doubt a very talented individual—and Pastor Jones is a well-respected member of the Parks and Recreation Board. But what if I were to tell you that Dr. John Doe's real name is Shane—the person who provided the achievement stories you just reviewed. You would want to carefully consider the nature of his giftedness as evidenced in the recurring themes of his achievement data. Then you would want to compare that evidence with the list of motivated abilities that should be criteria for selecting search committee members for any board or organization:

Critical Motivated Abilities for Search Committee Members

> Investigating: by interviewing, inquiring, gathering information

> Evaluating: by assessing worth, discerning, comparing to a standard

> Influencing: by initiating, gaining participation, persuading

> Communicating: by writing, explaining, listening

> Organizing: by setting direction and goals, defining tasks, establishing procedures

> Overseeing: by inspiring, leading, facilitating the work of others

Search Committee members should be motivated to work with people, individually and in groups, and to build relationships. They should also be motivated to work with data and information.

I am sure you will quickly recognize that Shane's achievements have very limited demonstration of the motivated abilities critical to performance on a search committee. The work and life achievements "Dr. Doe" most enjoyed and felt he did well provide valid and reliable behavioral evidence on which we can base our decision. With this kind of *evidence* about what he is really motivated to do, we are able to make an informed and accurate decision to decline his offer for candidacy. (Note: This is an actual case; "Dr. Doe" was most relieved that he was not selected to Chair the Search

Committee. He was only being "nice" to agree when asked by his pastor whether he would be willing to serve.)

To provide further insights into the evidence that can be gained in a MAP, let us review the work and life achievements prepared by Marty (another scientist) who was also nominated for the chair of this search committee. Marty was asked to write about his most meaningful achievements—those he enjoyed and felt he did well—from different stages of his life.

Marty's Achievement Data

Childhood—Playing Soccer

Set out to play soccer at school. I could see certain areas that I could learn fairly quickly—picked those areas, like learning to kick well. If you can become proficient, it is a big asset to the team. Watched my friends' strengths and weaknesses. I'd say "you point out what I'm doing wrong, and I'll point out what I see you doing wrong." We would gather together before the game and say "they've got stronger players, they're much more skilled than we are . . . but we can work together in a certain way and win." I would ask the guys for their observations about the players, and we would play out how we were going to work together. The most satisfying part was seeing the fruition of it all . . . a lot of fun.

Ages 23-26—Started a Testing Lab

Got interested in certain aspects of the project and wanted to try out some novel testing ideas. With a friend, we came up with some unique ideas for testing. Did "benchmarking" to check out the ideas then set up a testing company. Had a lot of satisfaction in running all aspects of the business. We developed a theory together; he was stronger theoretically, and I'd produce the testing results. We married the two together. Most satisfying to see I could do it: face problems, find out what they are thinking, persuade somebody. Got the ideas working and his career launched.

Age 40-47—Developed a New Sampling Method

I saw the need for a technical thing that could be developed, did my homework to check the market niche. Part of my job was to select technical ideas for development. I had to persuade our own people and work with the contractor to get the ideas accepted. After the sampling procedures were established, I put together a presentation and gave it to upper management. Satisfaction was in pushing that through and seeing that idea implemented.

To help you "add up" the evidence in Marty's achievement data, we have selected some key words and phrases. To emphasize the interrelationships within the components of the Motivated Abilities Pattern, the evidence is presented for each of the five parts:

Evidence	Theme
I would ask the guys, benchmarking, did my homework	Investigating
Could see certain areas, watched friends' strengths, checked out market niche	Evaluating
You point out—I'll point out, talked management into, persuaded,	Influencing
came up with friend's strengths and weaknesses . . . married the two together, picked someone I knew, he was stronger	Overseeing
I'd say, find out what they are thinking, put together a presentation	Communicating
Set out to, we can work together, procedures were established	Organizing

Subject Matter	Theme
someone I knew, my friend, team company, gather together	People
Science and Technology is also an important Subject Matter	

Circumstances	Theme
I could see areas that I could learn quickly, seeing that ideas were implemented	Growth, Potential

Operating Relationship	Theme
watched my friend's strengths and weaknesses, set up an interesting company, running all aspects of the business	Manager

Motivational Payoff	Theme
seeing the fruition of it, got the ideas working,	Bring to Completion
seeing the idea implemented	Reach the Objective

Marty's MAP includes some recurring evidence for nearly all of the criteria to become a member of the search committee. In addition, the achievement about playing soccer provides some additional evidence of a "match" to the mission of the Parks and Recreation Board. And Marty's motivational payoff to bring things to completion and reach an objective is frosting on the cake!

Once again, an informed and accurate decision can be made based on *recurring behavioral evidence*. The moral of this story—and this maxim applies to every selection and promotion decision—is that we simply cannot tell from a resume or a recommendation what a person is truly *motivated* to do. We must have evidence provided by the person's own description of what they enjoy doing and feel they do well, and that evidence must be reviewed by someone who knows what they are looking for!

In conclusion, it can be very misleading to base a selection decision on candidate information gleaned from degree level, major field of study, GPA, or years of experience. References and performance evaluations can be particularly misleading. A negative reference may really be a situation where a candidate was in a job that didn't "fit" his or her giftedness, and vice versa. The standard employment interview fails dramatically to uncover what the individual is truly motivated to do.

To achieve a high level of performance *and* personal fulfillment (read "employee retention") in any job, you have to use people whose giftedness matches the critical requirements of the job. To achieve this match, you need information about

> what the person is "motivated" to do
> and the critical motivations required for performing the job.

These two sets of information will form the basis for your search process.[4]

A complete explanation and discussion of Motivated Abilities can be found in *The Power of Uniqueness* by Arthur F. Miller Jr. with William Hendricks; *Managing Yourself, Managing Others* by Steven M. Darter; *Who Do You Think You Are?* by Nick Isbister and Martin Robinson; and *Passion and Purpose* by Marlys Hanson with Merle Hanson.

The Short List

8

HIGHLIGHTS

> **Preparing the short list**

> **Size of the short list**

> **Are there any skeletons in the candidate's closet?**

> **Learning more about the candidate**

PREPARING THE SHORT LIST

There will come a time in the sourcing process when you feel you have done a thorough job of getting the word out and the market has provided a good pool of candidates to work from. You have done your reference checking and have interviewed each candidate by phone, usually having several conversations with each. You have eliminated some candidates already and have mentally moved others forward. This is the time to formulate your short list.

Decide which candidates will be on your short list after interviewing *in person* each candidate who has been moved forward. From the short list, you can further narrow the pool and then name your final candidates. In most cases, your short list will be your list of final candidates.

SIZE OF THE SHORT LIST

What should be the size of the pool of candidates on your short list? Should you focus on only one candidate, or should

you have several on your short list and get to know them in-depth until one is clearly your best choice for the chief execu-tive officer position? There are differing opinions about this.

One theory is to move only one candidate forward at a time. Those who prefer this method refer to the process of having a short list of multiple candidates as a "beauty con-test." They talk about "parading the candidates in front of the search committee." Part of the argument for only having one candidate comes from the way some major corporations select their leaders and the way many colleges and profes-sional sports teams select their head coaches. In the case of sports, the athletic director and college president or the own-ers of the professional teams have their ideas and convictions about whom they would like to see as their head coach. In many instances, they go after this person until they get either a yes or no.

In the case of business, the process occasionally works as well. From the candidate's perspective, she knows that she is the only person the organization is considering. That sends a signal to her that there is a strong interest on the part of the organization. From the organization's perspective, they know that during this time period they have the candidate's undivided attention. The two parties can spend ample time getting to know each other.

I have never felt, however, that having only one or two candidates on the short list was in the best interest of the client. If the pool is strong enough, I like to have three to four people on the short list. This enables you to compare the strengths and flat spots of one candidate to a small pool of others. In addition, upon occasion, a search committee isn't totally clear on what they are looking for until they start interviewing people. Some just don't deal well in the abstract: interviewing and actually meeting the candidates and being able to "put flesh on paper" helps them clarify what they really want in their next CEO. So, unless there is someone in the pool that is so far superior to the others that, for all practical purposes, the decision has already been made, three to four is a good-sized pool.

Another risk associated with choosing only one candidate and dismissing the others is that you may offer the job to this candidate, only to have him decide that your top position is not his first choice. Certainly there are safeguards you can take to help ensure that this doesn't happen, but occasionally it will, and there are few things more frustrating than dismissing the other candidates on the short list, only to have your first choice not work out. Restarting the search is time consuming, and the fact that you are doing this indicates to the qualified and interested candidates that something went wrong in your initial search, which leads to questions and much explaining.

Making the decision on the next person to lead an organization is serious business. Having a variety of candidates helps you gain clarity on what you really want in your next chief executive officer, and it ensures that you will have a choice of final candidates should your first offer be declined. Now that you have your list of final candidates, you are almost ready to interview them face-to-face.

ARE THERE ANY SKELETONS IN THE CANDIDATE'S CLOSET?

As you narrow the pool of candidates to the short list, you must ask candid questions. Most veterans in the search business agree that before a candidate makes their short list, they are asked a question like "Are there any skeletons in your closet?" A more delicate way to ask would be "Is there anything in your background that would bring embarrassment to the client if it were known?" This is the best time to get these kinds of things out in the open, and this is the time to let the candidates know that you are going to conduct a very thorough screening of them.

Is there anything in your background that would bring embarrassment to the client if it were known?

If a candidate knows we are going to be talking to a number of people from a cross-section of his career history, he is more likely to come clean on things we should know. Part of the purpose in doing this is to let the candidate know just how comprehensive our screening process will be and that—if and when he makes the short list—we will know more about him than almost anyone else does. If there are things a candidate would rather not reveal, it is best to eliminate that person from consideration early in the process. If something potentially negative is revealed, however, it would not necessarily disqualify a candidate, depending upon the situation; it is just best that everything be known up front. The last thing the search committee wants is this type of surprise.

Learning More About the Candidate

There are a variety of ways to learn more about potential problems that may arise with your candidates, and ways to uncover positive traits she may not have thought to share with you as well. Here are some steps you should take to ensure a thorough understanding of your short list candidates:

Visit the Organization
Where the Candidate Currently Works

It is not uncommon, when searching for a new college president or nonprofit CEO, for a subcommittee of the search committee to visit the organization or campus where the candidate is currently employed. Of course, this needs to be done in cooperation with the candidate.

Verify Degrees

Much resume fraud occurs in the area of education. Some applicants claim degrees they didn't receive, a condition that's becoming more common. Consider the following incidents:

> Senator Joseph R. Biden, Jr. (D-Del) inflated his college academic credentials and borrowed from the speeches of a British politician to enhance his own.

> *Washington Post* reporter Janet Cooke inflated her academic record to get hired at the *Post*.

> Quincy Troupe, former California poet laureate and UC-San Diego professor, was well-respected within the California artist and academic community—until his lies about his college background were exposed.

> Sandra Baldwin, president of the United States Olympic Committee, resigned after it was revealed that she had lied about having a PhD in English from Arizona State University.

> Kenneth Lonchar, the CFO of Veritas, resigned after it was discovered in 2002 that he had lied about both his Stanford MBA and his undergraduate education.

> Marilee Jones was driven from her job as admissions director at MIT after twenty-eight years of presumably good service to the university. She had claimed a college degree she did not have when she applied for her job.

> David Edmondson resigned as chief executive officer of Radio Shack after it was discovered that he misstated his academic record. He had spent eleven years in a variety of jobs with the company, ultimately being named CEO.

> George O'Leary gets a dream job as football coach at University of Notre Dame and has to step down five days later because of resume lies. He claimed a master's degree and college football experience he didn't have.

This should be enough factual data to strongly encourage you to verify your applicant's academic degrees, and for that matter, other data from their resume.

READ THE CANDIDATE'S WRITING

Depending on the nature of your organization, you may find that some of your finalists have published books or articles that relate to their area of knowledge or the philosophy of your organization's mission. References to these publications may show up on their resume, or you might uncover them in a literature review. If anyone on your search committee has access to computerized literature programs such as Lexus-Nexus, ask him to see if he can find writings that might shed light on the candidate's management philosophy or give you an idea of what kind of CEO she might make.

Be sure to verify anything you read in the candidate's writing when you interview him or her. In Chapter 11 I discuss ways to avoid the "smile factor"—being sure your candidate is qualified and not just a great interviewee. This concept also applies to a candidate's writing; be sure they are as competent as they appear in their published works.

For instance, the world of books and journal articles is replete with material on management and leadership written by men and women who have a lot of head knowledge about management and leadership. These people have been able to get their books or journal articles published and are therefore considered by many to be experts in these areas. In reality, their expertise is in the topic itself and not necessarily in their ability to manage or lead an organization of any size.

Background Check

My company uses a national firm to conduct background investigations on all of our candidates. The money you spend for this is some of the best money you will spend in the search process.

Misconduct Self-Certification Statement

Some of our clients are religious organizations, and one of the mainline denominations we work with has a misconduct self-certification statement they require their ministers to submit when under consideration for a position. By signing this document, the person attests that there are no charges pending against them by the denomination or other legal authorities. This is not a sure-fire way to know that the person is honest, but is a good thing to do.

If you utilize something like this in your application process make sure you understand that by signing this, the candidate is only addressing things that have happened in the past. This document does not necessarily guarantee that the person has an absolutely clean record. A background check is still a good idea.

Checking
References

9

HIGHLIGHTS

> Reference checking is not a formality
> Collect second-party data
> Contextualize the candidate's experience
> Have I checked enough references?
> Contextualizing a reference's input
> Getting more and better references
> Beware of high-profile references
> Good reference checking takes time
> Get unbiased references

One of the most critical steps in the hiring process—reference checking—is often hurried or bypassed entirely. To obtain the best information from a candidate's references, the person conducting the reference check must carefully develop strategies to acquire this information.

Poor reference checking can be embarrassing. Technical incompetence when hiring a physician without valid credentials would be a major setback to a healthcare system. It would be a major embarrassment to most religious organizations if it were to come to light that the person they hired has a moral lapse in her background. Even less obvious red flags can come to light during a good reference check; thus it is imperative that you be thorough. In this chapter, you have

information that will help you develop strategies and improve your ability to conduct a thorough reference interview.

REFERENCE CHECKING IS NOT A FORMALITY

In many cases, checking references is viewed as a mere formality, and if so, it is often one of the last things to be done in the hiring process, generally for confidentiality reasons. If you have candidates who are serving another organization in a highly visible position, they probably will ask that you be very discreet regarding those with whom you will speak. In cases like these, you must honor the candidate's request, but the candidate must also realize that there will come a time when his candidacy becomes more public and that you will need to do a thorough reference check at that point.

To get the best data, however, reference checking actually should be a part of your qualifying process from the very beginning—when you decide that the person you have interviewed has the qualifications to be a viable candidate. At this point, you can do a preliminary reference check—the more formal reference interview can come later. When I do a preliminary reference check, I call people in my network who have had contact with the candidate over the years. I ask general questions about his character and work ethic. You might find that it saves time to e-mail the reference your questions and ask them to respond to you via e-mail. You can use these responses to determine if you want to spend some time with that reference.

Reference checking Is not a formality.

In the more formal reference interview, I develop questions from the Critical Position Requirements. Both interview settings will be discussed further in this chapter.

The candidates should know that before they make it to the short list, a systematic and thorough check of their references will be done. Knowing that you will be conducting thorough reference checking will often encourage them to be more honest and open with you in response to your questions.

COLLECT SECOND-PARTY DATA

In many cases, the way someone's name gets into our search pool is by submission from a friend or peer. This is a good time to ask the person submitting the name preliminary reference check questions. Oftentimes, you will know people within your network who have worked with the potential candidate. You can call these people to ask them the general questions as well.

> ❯ How long have you known John?
> ❯ In what context have you known him?
> ❯ What is his work ethic like?

In addition, ask specific questions related to his behavior, which you will garner from reading the candidate's resume. For example, if her resume says that she led the organization through significant change, ask:

> ❯ What was going on in the organization that caused the needed change?
> ❯ How did she lead?
> ❯ Can you give me a specific example?
> ❯ What was the aftermath of her change process?

Or the CPRs might state that you are looking for someone who can "build relationships with a large board." In that case you would ask,

> ❯ What was her relationship like with your board?
> ❯ How did she build a relationship with them?

Questions like these will often bring to light something about the candidate you didn't already know. Take the time to explore that and see where it leads. Every time you talk with

someone who knows the candidate, try to work through these questions. Each person might not have a response to all of the questions, but if you ask them of enough people, a pattern will emerge.

CONTEXTUALIZE THE CANDIDATE'S EXPERIENCE

One question you should ask someone who is referring a candidate is how the person compares to others they have known in the same or very similar positions. You might say, "If selected as chief executive officer of our organization, John will need very strong strategic planning skills. How would you rate his strategic planning ability in relation to other nonprofit chief executive officers you have known?"

> One question you should ask someone who is referring a candidate is how the person compares to others they have known in the same or very similar positions.

Forcing the reference to think of the candidate in the context of other top leaders causes him to focus his response. If he describes John as having great strategic planning skills, but then compares him to other nonprofit chief executive officers as average, that gives you a more meaningful perspective. Looking at things in context always makes the information more useful.

HAVE I CHECKED ENOUGH REFERENCES?

As I have already mentioned, in the initial stages of every search I conduct, it is customary to spend a lot of time getting to know the organization and their expectations for the person we have been retained to hire. On one such occasion, I was talking to the chairman of the board of my client organization, and I could tell he was a bit distraught. He started by saying that he had been the head of the search committee that had selected their last president. This man had lasted less than three years, and in the eyes of several trustees, had been a dismal failure.

Among the many things he shared with me that afternoon was how the references had been checked, which he had taken personal responsibility for. He only checked two references, and these were from two people for whom he had high regard. One was a nationally renowned university professor who had taught the candidate in graduate school. The other was a prominent attorney whom my client knew through another board on which they served together. Both of these men knew the candidate well and gave him glowing recommendations.

As my client reflected on what went wrong, he commented that he had learned several things from this unpleasant incident. One was that he didn't check enough references. Unless the candidate is well known by the organization and its board members, it is highly unlikely that two references are sufficient to give a proper "read" on the candidate.

The other lesson he learned, which is probably the most important, is to take into consideration the context in which the person making the recommendation knows the candidate. In this case, the professor had known the candidate well as a student—thirty years prior—and had followed the candidate's career from afar. He did not have any first-hand knowledge of the candidate's recent leadership experience and had never seen him in a managerial or leadership capacity.

The attorney only knew the candidate in the context of serving on another board with him. In this case, he saw the candidate two to three times a year, and not in the candidate's vocational setting. Consequently, neither of these men knew the candidate in the context of his current work.

My client went on to lament that his reference checking would have been much more meaningful if he had taken the time to contact several people, particularly some who had first-hand experience or knowledge of the candidate in his current position.

So how do you get enough good references to believe that you have completed this part of the due diligence on the

candidates? Where do you get these references? One recruiter that I know asks the candidate for three references from the past five positions that he has held. He wants the name and contact data of the person's immediate supervisor, one of his peers, and one of his subordinates. He also tells the candidate that if he makes the short list, that there will be much more extensive reference checking. If the candidate flinches at this idea, that might give you an idea if there is anything in her background that she doesn't want you to know about.

CONTEXTUALIZING A REFERENCE'S INPUT

For the past several years, 360-degree interviewing has been in vogue in many human resources circles. A similar technique can be used when checking someone's references. It is a good idea to talk to people who have supervised the person, who have worked for the person (subordinates), and who have been working peers of the candidate. In my experience you can also get very useful reference data from people who have known the candidate outside the work environment, but I have found that interviewing references who have worked with the candidates gives us the most helpful information. It is critical to interview at least one person in each of these categories: supervisors, peers, and subordinates. Ask the candidate to provide you with the names and contact information of these people.

If you choose to use a candidate's friend as a reference, be careful. They may have a difficult time being objective. But the most important reason not to use a candidate's friends as references is that they may not know that much about the candidate's work habits. After all, your reference questions will be designed to discover if the candidate can meet your Critical Position Requirements, and if the reference has never worked with the candidate, he will be unable to answer most of your questions. About all he can give you is a character reference.

As you decide how much weight to give to the input of each reference, you should consider the strength and depth of the relationship that the reference has with the candidate. Input from someone who has worked with the person over time is usually more valuable than that coming from a short-term relationship.

GETTING MORE AND BETTER REFERENCES

Getting a good list of references from a candidate may be difficult for a variety of reasons: it may be hard to reach a particular reference, candidates may list references that they have not worked with in a number of years, or they may be reluctant to list references with whom they currently work for confidentiality reasons. There is a way, however, both to get a larger number of references and to get quality references. One of my clients taught me to ask candidates to provide organizational charts from her three most recent jobs. Through these charts, you can learn two important things about the candidate:

Make sure the candidate knows that you will be checking other references, in addition to the ones he provided.

1. You can learn where your candidate ranked in the context of her previous job. This gives you an impression of the breadth of her previous responsibilities.

2. You can obtain the names of people who were peers, subordinates, or supervisors of a candidate. If you're having a hard time getting references, ask permission to talk with these people.

Proper reference checking can help companies hire people who will thrive in the organization. As a result, more time can be spent getting things done, and less time has to be spent dealing with the results of a poor hiring decision. It is

a lose-lose situation when a bad hiring decision is made, and thorough reference checking can help ensure that your hiring decision is a good one.

BEWARE OF HIGH-PROFILE REFERENCES

Occasionally someone will provide the name of a high-profile public person as a reference. Unless I know from personal experience or reliable third-party conversation that the candidate has more than a passing relationship with the celebrity, I don't go to a lot of trouble to contact them, nor do I have high expectations about what I am likely to hear.

High-profile public figures are usually very difficult to contact, and if you do make contact with them, you are not likely to get them to have a conversation of much length or depth because they generally don't have a great deal of time to give you. Also, someone of this stature is not likely to make any negative comments about the person, even if they are true. And in many cases, the high-profile reference only has a general knowledge of the candidate— not a working relationship.

Beware of high-profile references.

GOOD REFERENCE CHECKING TAKES TIME

If you make contact with someone and they only have a few minutes at that time or seem rushed, it is best to ask them if you can schedule a time when they have forty-five minutes to an hour to talk.

What is the best time and place to contact a reference? For some, the only place you are going to be able to contact them is at their office. However, if you are able to talk with the reference when they are at home, they are more likely to be at ease and you will probably learn more about your candidate.

Some people find it helpful to spend the first few minutes of the interview making a personal connection. Before you call think about things you might ask: have you ever visited their city? are there acquaintances or friends you have in common? do they have a professional or college sports team in their city that you can talk about?

Taking the time to get to know your reference, even just a little bit, puts her more at ease, and she will be much more likely to give you in-depth information if she feels comfortable with you.

GET UNBIASED REFERENCES

There is a tendency for the person conducting the search to get attached to the finalists. The candidates on the short list have survived a rigorous search process. In all likelihood, chairman of the search has spent many hours getting to know these people—on the telephone, in person, and has possibly even met their spouses. It can be easy to lose objectivity. To avoid this level of bias, have another person from your search committee conduct the reference checks.

Having the Board Chairman Check the References

There are those who would argue that no matter how busy you are, the person making the hire should personally contact all references. In the case of a board-conducted search, this is probably the board's chairman. Their argument is that the person making the hiring decision knows which skills and operational styles are best for the organization and the position. Also, since most of the references are likely to be the candidate's former supervisors, it can be easier to establish rapport between these peers.

In fact, as a rule I have found it helpful when the person checking the reference is a vocational peer with the person giving the reference. For example:

> ❯ When I am doing a search for a college or university president and the candidate lists a faculty member at

his current school as a reference, I ask a faculty member on the search committee to check this reference.

> If the candidate lists a trustee or board member of his current employer as a reference, I ask one of the trustees or board members of the search committee to check this reference.

Having a Professional Check the References

Early in my career as a search professional, I learned that I did not have all of the skills or the levels of passion and energy necessary to conduct adequately every element of the search process. I have grown to appreciate the value of utilizing people in areas in which they have core competencies, natural talent, and passion for specific types of work I cannot or would prefer not to complete.

I have seen this bear out repeatedly in my experience with reference checking. Late one afternoon, one of my associates came to me and said that a person she had called to check a reference had paid her a compliment. The person she had called was a trial lawyer, and when our associate had telephoned him, she had asked, in her usual manner, if he had thirty to forty-five minutes to talk. He had said that he was in a hurry, but wanted to help and so she continued with the reference check then. After the discussion was complete, he had told our associate that she would make a good trial lawyer. She had responded that she wasn't sure that was a compliment, but none the less, had thanked him and asked "why did he think so?" Apparently, he was quite impressed by her ability to "disarm" him and put him at ease very early in the conversation, which allowed her to get more information from him than he normally would have disclosed. He had told her that as a rule, he only gave very brief and rather nondescript responses to reference questions. It was obvious that our associate had a real knack for putting people at ease and getting what she needed in her time on the phone.

A good reference checker will have a natural ability to ask gentle, probing questions, getting more than surface responses. While there certainly are skills involved, this is really an art form. Far too many people will settle for a shallow initial response and do not probe for more significant and useful data. Thorough reference checking requires time, patience, and the ability to probe deeply, not accepting surface responses for an answer. If you are not skilled in these areas, you should consider having a professional conduct the references for you.

If your reference questions are formulated to correspond with your Critical Position Requirements, if you have a good list of references that encompasses the candidate's supervisors, peers, and subordinates, if you take the time to probe deeply during your reference interviews, and if you have the ability to put the person you are interviewing at ease, you will come away from your reference checks with a more thorough knowledge of each of your candidates. This knowledge will be one of the factors you will use in making your final decision as to whom to hire as your next chief executive officer.

It is obvious from this chapter that checking references is not an exact science. I encourage each search committee to have a good discussion about how they can work together as a team to get the best information possible from the formal reference checking.

The Internal Candidate

10

HIGHLIGHTS

> Some realities about internal candidates
> Does the internal candidate automatically make the short list?
> The internal candidate and the interview process
> Are you using the external candidate as fodder?
> How will internal candidates impact the overall quality of the pool?
> Special note for college and university president searches

Often current employees or board members of the organization will surface as internal candidates for the available chief executive officer position. Sometimes the names of these people will be introduced at the beginning of the search, but frequently I have uncovered internal candidates as I have done the front-end work on the search, usually when writing the Opportunity Profile or the Critical Position Requirements. Promoting an internal candidate can often be beneficial for your organization if the candidate truly outshines the others in the pool.

Evaluating internal versus external candidates doesn't have to be a race. You should not have the attitude of pitting one against the other. Rather, the goal should be to get the best person in the job, regardless of where she comes from.

There is a school of thought that claims all other things being equal, the internal candidate is the best choice. The reasoning behind this is that you have a better idea of the internal

candidate's weaknesses, so you can plan for them. With the outside candidate, you probably aren't quite as confident that you know his weaknesses. In the words of Fortunat Mueller-Maerki, a partner with Egon Zehnder International, "a known risk is a smaller risk than an unknown one because it is manageable."[5]

There are some cautions to observe, however, when conducting a search that includes internal candidates. First, I will discuss some of the pitfalls.

SOME REALITIES ABOUT INTERNAL CANDIDATES

Many people inside your organization will have seen the internal candidate in a number of situations over a period of years. These circumstances will vary—formal, informal, making presentations, dealing with critics, gaining consensus, and so on. This can make the consideration and evaluation of the internal candidate *seem* easier to members of the search committee.

If your organization has a fairly traditional culture, it will most likely be difficult not to choose the internal candidate. Unless the other candidates are unbelievably strong or bring something to the organization for which there is currently a severe deficiency, a vote for an outside candidate, even if you are looking for change and new ideas, will be difficult. Someone once said this is the case of "the devil we know versus the devil we don't know." There can be a lot of truth to this.

If the internal candidate has been doing a good job in his current position and, for the most part, is well liked and respected, many people will have a difficult time selecting someone from the outside over this person, as they will feel that hiring the outside candidate is a vote against the internal one. And some people may go so far as to think that since the internal candidate has been loyal to the organization and has been doing a good job in his present position, he has *earned the right* to be the next chief executive officer of the organization. Occasionally, you will meet resistance from significant donors and other stakeholders as well. These people might have strong ties to the internal candidates, or they may think you are wasting time and the organization's money (if you have retained a search firm) by even considering external candidates.

My counsel in these cases is that you should always return to the Opportunity Profile (to reference the functional requirements necessary for the chief executive officer) and to the Critical Position Requirements (to reference the motivational behaviors we want in the next chief executive officer) in order to focus on factors that are critical to success in the position.

This is not to say that members of the search committee should not value loyalty and commitment to the organization. They are of crucial importance but do not categorically give an employee an automatic promotion.

DOES THE INTERNAL CANDIDATE AUTOMATICALLY MAKE THE SHORT LIST?

Should internal candidates automatically be put on the short list, or should they go through the sourcing competition to see if they rise to the top as a finalist? You can proceed with your search either way.

Fast Track to the Short List

In some searches, the board will say that they would like certain people to automatically make the short list. In this case you need to listen carefully and even "read between the lines" of what is really being said.

What they may be saying is that, at this time, the internal candidate will be hired unless they can be convinced otherwise. If this is the case, it becomes the task of the search committee to come up with candidates whose credentials, experience, and motivational compatibility to the CPRs make them as good or better choices than the internal candidate.

Or, the board could be saying that it would be political suicide not to have the internal candidates on the short list.

There may be a real or perceived danger of losing these people as employees if they are not elevated to the top position or at least given serious consideration.

Another message they may be sending is that certain key financial contributors to the organization want the internal candidates on the short list. This can be a sticky area and needs to be handled with care.

A way to give the search process credibility is to put internal candidates into the sourcing funnel and through the same rigor as external candidates. If, over time, they compete with others, end up on the short list, and one is then selected as the new leader, her leadership is much more legitimate.

THE INTERNAL CANDIDATE AND THE INTERVIEW PROCESS

As stated earlier, there are at least two different types of internal candidates: employees of the organization (such as the executive vice president or other senior leaders), and board members for the organization.

The internal candidate has an advantage in the interview process. Search committee members probably know the person or are at least somewhat familiar with her work. She has made a significant impact or contribution to the organization, or she would not be on the short list in the first place.

Also, because the internal candidate is obviously more familiar with the organization, she will be better prepared for the interview, and the illustrations and stories she tells during the interview will appear to be more relevant. In this situation, there is a tendency to elevate the candidate, because she is perceived to know more about the organization. The truth is, she does know more about the organization—she works there every day!

To give credibility to the process, the search committee must work hard to initially evaluate the internal candidates against the standard of what a person must possess to excel in the position (based on the Opportunity Profile and the

Critical Position Requirements). Only after that evaluation and assessment has been made should the candidates be evaluated against each other.

ARE YOU USING THE EXTERNAL CANDIDATE AS FODDER?

In my experience, searches that include internal candidates almost always inspire the outside candidates to ask at some point during the sourcing process, "Am I cannon fodder in this search?" Organizations must be careful not to get the reputation of using external candidates merely to validate the internal candidate. If this happens too often, the observing public will get wise to this, and over time, it will become increasingly more difficult for your organization to attract good talent from the outside. Potential candidates will be checking out your organization as diligently as you are probing the backgrounds of the candidates. They will talk to their contacts who have knowledge of your organization, and the reputation, good or bad, of how you have handled searches in the past, as well as how you run your organization, will be spread. Thus you want to ensure that your search is conducted without reproach.

The difficulty of attracting good talent from the outside seems to be particularly true for institutions of higher education. When you get to the number of candidates who, at any given time, are qualified and ready to move into the presidency position at a college or university, you are usually dealing with a small number of people. To quote one applicant, "This is a small fraternity. We all know each other, and none of us wants to be the bridesmaid too many times."

HOW WILL INTERNAL CANDIDATES IMPACT THE QUALITY OF THE POOL?

Having internal candidates can definitely impact the quality of the pool.

> ❯ How strong is the internal candidate?
> ❯ How well is this person known outside of the organization?

If you have a strong internal candidate and this person has a good reputation outside of the organization, it could make it difficult to attract other strong external candidates. More often than not, if there is a perceived strong internal candidate, many outside candidates will tell me that they think the internal candidate is going to get the job and that the search is just window dressing by the Board to give the impression that they are conducting a national search. It is often difficult to convince them otherwise.

I am a strong proponent of promoting from within, as long as that person rises to the top of the pool on a level playing field. However, I am quick to counsel Boards that if they have a strong internal candidate, the pool may not be as strong as it might otherwise be.

SPECIAL NOTE FOR COLLEGE AND UNIVERSITY PRESIDENT SEARCHES

As I mentioned, when you serve on a search committee to find the next president of a college or university, you are generally dealing with a fairly finite number of candidates. This is particularly true if your college or university has a regional reputation or some other niche that would narrow the list of candidates.

In these cases, you need to pay particular attention to the internal candidates. Some would argue that if you have strong internal candidates, you should seek them out and evaluate them against your CPRs before you go outside. If you are convinced that you have your person in the internal pool, you can save the search committee a lot of work and possible bad press in the academic community if you go ahead and make your selection.

Let me illustrate with an example from a search I observed but did not conduct. The school was a first-tier liberal arts college. When the search began, it didn't appear that there would be any internal candidates. Many people believed that this made it easier to assemble a strong pool of external candidates. As the search progressed, the pool was narrowed to three people.

The word on the street was that the search process had been very rigorous. The external candidates had been put through a very intense interview process that had included multiple interviews. To most outsiders observing the search, it appeared that the process was moving toward selection of one of the external candidates. At the very end of the process, however, someone from the inside decided that he would enter the search. This person was a strong candidate and was ultimately selected for the position.

Although, to my knowledge, none of the external candidates said anything in public about the search process's being unfair, it was common knowledge that a couple of them felt that way. During this same timeframe, I was conducting a search on behalf of another college. I thought one of the candidates who was not selected for the position at the liberal arts school might be a good match for my search, so I initiated a call. I got nowhere with this person. She said that she had been burned so badly in the other search, that she would be very hesitant to get involved in another search for at least a year, if not longer, particularly if such a search involved internal candidates.

The bad public relations that this college brought upon itself were significant. By allowing the internal candidate to enter at the last minute and not putting that candidate through the same rigor that each of the external candidates had experienced, the college had earned a dose of justifiable skepticism from the public that will be around for several years. And the ripple effect of this negative reaction affected other institutions doing their searches as well.

I would therefore urge you to be cautious when considering internal candidates. In some cases, they may be the best
for your organization. Just be sure to put them through the
same rigorous process that you would any external candidate,
and you will be able to avoid any hint of impropriety in the
long run, and your search process will remain a credible one.

Interviewing the Final Candidates

11

HIGHLIGHTS

> Treating the candidates with dignity
> Preparing the candidates for the interviews
> Beware of the "smile factor"
> Are you getting useful data?
> Behavioral interviewing
> How to interview the candidates
> Where should you conduct the interviews?
> Interview formats

The search committee has worked very hard. The cream has risen to the top. You think that you have your next CEO in this group of finalists, and the time has come to spend more in-depth time with these candidates. Now is not the time to rush the process, but rather to take the time to learn more about the candidates. This chapter will give you some pointers that should come in handy in your search.

TREATING THE CANDIDATES
WITH DIGNITY

While writing this manuscript, one day I was flying to St. Louis to interview a candidate. It happened that someone I had found for a position as the president of a college was on that flight. Five years had passed since he had been made president, so we had some catching up to do.

After we spent a few minutes catching up with each other, the topic turned to my book project. Naturally he was interested, so I shared parts of the manuscript with him. He asked if he could share some thoughts with me on his recollections and perceptions of the interview process. For the most part it had been a good experience for him. However, he remembered one thing that was a bit unsettling to him: the search committee had brought all three candidates to campus to be interviewed on the same day. He said that made him feel like a commodity. It was a bit awkward being there with the other two candidates. He thought they all would have felt better about the process if they had been brought in on separate days and given more personal attention. As it was, he said it felt very impersonal.

As we talked he asked me if I remembered the rationale for having the three candidates there on the same day. My response was that if the search committee has to bring its members to the interviews from different geographical areas, it is more cost effective to cluster the interviews or to have them back-to-back as opposed to staging them a week apart. He agreed that it was the most cost-effective way to conduct interviews, but it wasn't the most emotionally settling for the candidates.

Over the next few days I reflected upon this. I went so far as to check with candidates from other searches I had conducted. The majority of these people felt the same way.

Since then I have been careful to share this perception with search committees. For economic reasons most committees choose to cluster the interviews, but some have taken this man's thoughts to heart and made sure that all the candidates were not at the same place at the same time.

PREPARING THE CANDIDATES FOR THE INTERVIEWS

When you are ready to interview your short list of candidates, you need to give these people the best possible opportunity for success in the interview. If they have not already requested it, you should offer certain information and ask the candidates what other information they need in order to be fully prepared for the interview. The following is a list of material and information that is frequently requested by candidates prior to the interviews:

> the long-range or strategic plan for your organization
> a description of the process used in developing the long-range or strategic plan
> the audited financial reports from the last two years
> any marketing or strategic planning audits
> any external or peer reviews
> the IRS Form 990 reports from the last two years
> the organizational chart
> the job descriptions of the top people on the executive team
> biographic data on the members of the interview team

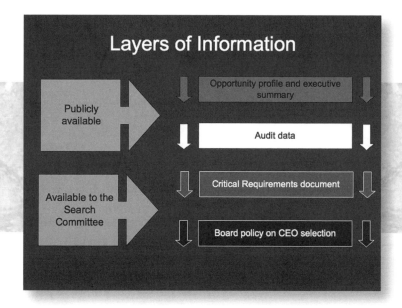

Depending upon your organization, you may be asked for other material as well. While some material is sensitive and your natural inclination may be to use discretion in whom you allow to see it, this is not the time to hold back. For both parties to make the best decision possible, the candidates need to get to know your organization as well as you are getting to know them.

Remember that an interview is a two way street—a dialogue, not a monologue. Not only are you trying to ascertain information from the candidates about themselves, but you must also allow time for the candidates to question you about your organization and how it operates. Remember, in addition to garnering information from the candidates, you are trying to "sell" your organization to them. The candidate is putting her best foot forward. You must remember to do the same. You are still in a selling mode until you make the hire.

> **Remember that an interview is a two way street—a dialogue, not a monologue.**

BEWARE OF THE "SMILE FACTOR"

For the most part, the people who make your short list will have a good interview. Chances are they will be rather persuasive. You would expect this, because the individuals you want to interview would not have gotten this far in their careers without having reasonably good influencing and persuading skills.

> **Beware of the "Smile Factor." Competency to do a job and the ability to sell oneself are not the same thing.**

This is where you have to be very careful. Competency to do a job and the ability to sell oneself are not the same thing. Unfortunately, when it comes to making hiring decisions, the individuals doing the interviewing and hiring frequently fail to make this distinction. The result? The two are often confused. The person with more polish than substance is often hired, and the selection process fails to find the best person for the job.

There are a number of areas you can examine to ensure that your candidate is not simply sliding by on their good persuasion skills but is actually competent to fulfill your board's desires for the chief executive officer position.

Professional and Technical Skills

In any hiring situation, there are several factors to evaluate. The first has to do with professional or technical skills, functional experience, and competency. For example:

> Has the candidate paid his dues? Has he risen through the ranks and had enough varied experience to learn the profession?

> Does she have the skills and experience necessary to do the job?

> Does he know his stuff? Is his experience superficial or does he really know the field?

Style

Another area to evaluate is how the person puts his or her technical/functional experience to use; in a word, what is his "style." Skills, experience, and technical competency are fairly easy to observe and evaluate. And people rarely fail in a job because of inadequate skills or a lack of technical or functional competency. The individual's style is far more difficult to determine. Good hiring is all about expectations. Failure in job fit is almost always a result of one's style—not doing the job in a manner that pleases the board.

Some organizations may desire very different qualities in their chief executive officers. Earlier you read about the candidate for university president whose primary focus was on building and maintaining relationships with external constituents, whereas the board wanted him to place primary focus on on-campus activities. The candidate was well qualified for the position, but his leadership style was not what the board desired.

You must ask yourself the following questions: Is your organization used to a style of leadership that involves many people giving input before the CEO makes a decision? Or is your organization used to a more autocratic style, in which the chief executive officer makes all the decisions with little or no input and then expects those decisions to be implemented without question? Depending on what the board wants in these kinds of "cultural" issues, a particular individual's style may or may not be good fit for a your organization's top position.

A final aspect of style is how the person interacts with the board. If the board is used to providing a high degree of guidance and direction to the previous chief executive officer but ends up selecting a "lone wolf" who operates independently, this can present significant challenges. On the other hand, hiring a person who expects and depends on that level of direction from the board in an organization used to having its chief executive officer operate with a high degree of autonomy can also present great difficulty.

Knowing what kind of leadership style your board is looking for will help you determine if a particular candidate is right for you. This should be established when you write the CPRs for the job. Thus when you are interviewing your final candidates, be sure to ask specific questions that will give you a picture of their leadership in action.

Reference Consistency

A third area to consider is the references, which I discussed in Chapter 9. During your interview with each final candidate, you can ask some of the same questions that you asked of the candidate's reference to determine consistency. If the questions correspond to the CPRs and are thorough, then the information you learned from the references should be consistent with what you have observed in the candidate's resume and interviews.

Chemistry

Finally, you must consider "chemistry." How well do you like the person? As a board member, would you be comfortable serving the organization during this person's time of leadership? How does the Chairman of the Board feel about the chemistry? After all, she will be the one spending the most time with your new CEO.

All four of these areas should be given strong consideration as the search committee goes through the final interview process. The candidates' performances in each area—experience, style, reference consistency, and chemistry—will determine the outcome of the search.

ARE YOU GETTING USEFUL DATA?

After name, rank, and serial number, where do you go in an interview? What questions should be asked? How do you determine how the candidate will perform once on the job?

An interview is only as good as the interviewer's ability to ask the right questions. Unless you can reliably translate information from an interview into predictable behavior on the job, the questions you ask are useless. You need a process—or at least a sound rationale—for analyzing information to arrive at a valid conclusion about how this individual will likely perform in your organization.

> **An interview is only as good as the interviewer's ability to ask the right questions.**

In the following sections, you will discover how to ask substantive questions and how to evaluate the answers to those questions.

BEHAVIORAL INTERVIEWING

I have been in several interviews that included questions such as: "If you were hired for this position, how would you . . .?" or "What would you do if . . .?" This is not the way

to frame a question to get the most helpful response. Over the past forty-five years, my colleagues and I have collectively interviewed over six hundred thousand people, and we have learned that you get the most helpful data when you focus on specifics that the candidate has done in his past.

Aristotle once said, "We are what we repeatedly do. Excellence, then, is not an act but a habit." Our experience bears this out: knowing what the candidate has done in the past will predict how she will perform in the future. You want to ask questions, therefore, about what she has done and how she has performed in her past positions. This is behavioral interviewing.

Behavioral interviewing can be extremely useful when there are two candidates who are very close in the selection process. In these cases, having knowledge of how the candidates have performed in the past is very helpful.

Examples of Behavioral Interviewing

In this section, I will give you several quotes from candidates' resumes, and will show you how to ask questions, based on the candidates' behaviors, in order to ascertain what those statements really mean. Look for action verbs in the resumes that relate to the areas you want to explore. Circle these action verbs and ask probing questions around what the individual was doing during this time.

Sample quote from a candidate's resume: "Established the first offices, oversaw the incorporation, copyrighting, trademarking and registration of training programs and courses, and managed all administration and development for the organization."

To get the most from this statement, you might ask the candidate questions such as these:

> ⟩ When you say you "established the first offices," what was your role in this?

> If I had been with you during this time, what would I have seen you doing?

> How many other people were involved? How did you interface with them?

> What was your specific role in each of the responsibilities you listed? How did you go about this?

Sample quote from a candidate's resume: "Eliminated a $2 million operating loss and achieved profitability ahead of plan."

Suggested line of questioning:

> When you were the chief executive officer of XYZ organization, you "eliminated a $2 million operating loss and achieved profitability ahead of plan."

> Tell me about your role in this particular accomplishment. What was your specific contribution? How did you go about this?

> What size staff did you have? What direct involvement did any of these people have in this achievement?

Sample quote from a candidate's resume: "Increased annual revenue from $70,000 to more than $3,000,000."

Suggested line of questioning:

> When you were executive director of XYZ organization, you "increased annual revenue from $70,000 to more than $3,000,000." That's quite an accomplishment. Tell us, how long did it take you to do that? Specifically, how did you do this?

> If members of this committee had been with you during this time, what specific things might we have seen you do?

Sample quote from a candidate's resume: "Increased market coverage from four counties to more than 60 percent of the state."

Suggested line of questioning:

> When you "increased market coverage from four counties to more than 60 percent of the state," specifically what did *you* do to achieve this level of coverage?

> How many counties were in your state?

Sample quote from a candidate's resume: "Reduced staff turnover by 25 percent through creative scheduling. Increased productivity with fewer staff through targeted incentives."

Suggested line of questioning:

> Turnover is always a big thing with any nonprofit. How did you go about "reducing staff turnover by 25 percent through creative scheduling?"

> Tell me what you mean by "creative scheduling."

> Tell us about the time when you "increased productivity with fewer staff through targeted incentives." What was your specific role in this?

> How much were you able to decrease the level of staffing? How did the staff respond to this?

> Tell us about the "targeted incentive" program.

Hopefully, you can see from these examples how this line of questioning will give you a better picture of how the person is likely to perform when he becomes your chief executive officer. **Remember, don't ask what he would do; rather explore and probe into what he has done.** As you listen to a candidate, watch for correlations between what the person has done and what you want him to do at your organization. Remember that you want to use the interview time to catch a glimpse of the person in action. Question, listen, and evaluate. Don't try to read anything into what they are saying; just listen and summarize.

HOW TO INTERVIEW THE CANDIDATES

How long should the interviews last, and how many interviews does it take to get to the point at which you know the candidate well enough to make an offer? It is difficult to make a hiring decision from the amount of information you can gather in only one interview. All too often, I have seen search committees attempt to make their decision after a brief and hurried two-hour interview. It is simply very difficult to know enough about a person to make a quality decision from only one interview.

The following phases are suggestions for how you should allocate your time during the interview, regardless of how much time you have.

Phase One

This is your opportunity to talk about your organization. If you are taking the lead position in the interviews (that is, you are the first one interviewing the candidates), you should start with introductory comments to put the candidate at ease and get things going. Take about one quarter of the allotted time to accomplish this important task.

If you are not the lead interviewer, share information about your position and responsibilities within the organization. Look for opportunities to confirm your confidence in and enthusiasm for your organization.

Phase Two

This is the part of the interview for questioning, listening, and evaluating. The candidate should do most of the talking. Be prepared by having read the resume or the evaluation criteria and find the areas that generate interest in your mind. Start with a general question that will give the candidate an

opening to get him or her talking. Phase two should take about one half of the time scheduled.

Opening with one of the following:

"Tell us about yourself."

"What should we know about you?"

Ask the above questions only if you are the first interviewer to talk with the candidate. You don't want to waste valuable time making the candidate answer the same questions more than once.

If the candidate says something that calls for a follow-up question, make a note. Don't interrupt; listen and think. When there is a pause, ask your follow-up question. Then move your questions to a more specific level. Focus on the candidate's verbs or action statements. Tie your questions to specifics; avoid the philosophical questions like, "Tell me about client service." After you have asked some specific follow-up questions, add one or two from the following list, if time remains.

> "What are your weaknesses?"

> "Why are you drawn to this position?"

> "What are the critical factors you will use to decide whether or not to join our organization?"

> "What kind of work culture do you want to work in?"

> "What passion motivates you at work?"

Phase Three

Now it is time to ask the candidate for her questions. There are many great opportunities to assess the candidate by analyzing her questions.

> "What can I tell you; what questions do you have for me?"

In Chapter 8 I talked about finding out if there are any skeletons in the closet of the candidate. A smart candidate will take this opportunity to ask you, "Are there any skeletons in the organization's closet?". If the candidate has done his due diligence and has reason to believe there are skeletons in your closet, he will phrase the question "What are the skeletons in your organization's closet?"

If you haven't already done so, now is the time to come clean with any problem areas that the next chief executive officer will have to face. It is better to get these things on the table now than to have the chief executive officer surprised when he gets into the job.

As you respond to the candidate's questions, remember to continue to be a "promoter" for your organization. Phase three should take about one quarter of the time scheduled.

Phase Four

The final phase of the interview process is the wrap up. Here you can finish the interview on a high point. After finding out if there is any additional information that the candidate needs or if she has questions to ask, look for an opportunity to make a transitional statement, such as, "Well, Jane, this has been a good interview. Thanks so much for investing the time to come to be with us. We have learned a lot and think you are a fine candidate."

Collect Your Thoughts

As soon as you have said goodbye to the candidate, take a quiet moment to collect your thoughts and impressions. You will soon be back in the flow of your day, and you don't want to miss the ideas and impressions you have had. If you have a formal evaluation form, use it to collect the impressions. Make some short notes to help you remember.

> What was your overall impression of the candidate?

> Does he look the part?

> Is her experience a general match?

> Is his education a match?

> Did she describe situations that had the gifts you are looking for?

> What were his questions like? What do they tell you?

> Is the candidate mature enough to handle your situation?

Remember that you are looking for evidence that he can do the job successfully; you are not looking for perfection.

WHERE SHOULD YOU CONDUCT THE INTERVIEWS?

I have used a variety of venues to conduct interviews with candidates. Some search committees choose to interview on site. They understand this gives the candidates a feel for the organization. I have also used conference rooms at major hotels. Some have "living room" type spaces that are more comfortable and less formal than conference rooms. I have conducted off-site interviews in lodges and other informal settings. And I have conducted interviews in the homes of members of the search committee.

While good arguments can be made for each of the locations mentioned above, our best experiences have been when a member of the search committee had a home large enough to comfortably conduct the interviews. There is something about the informality of meeting in someone's home that creates an environment conducive for getting to know people.

INTERVIEW FORMATS

What interview format should you use?

> Interview by entire search committee

> Interview by round-robin approach

Interview by Entire Search Committee

The size of the search committee and the time that each person has for the interview process will be a major factor in determining the interview format. I have conducted searches in which the entire committee wanted to interview each candidate. One advantage of this format is that each member of the search committee hears the same thing from each candidate, and there is not much need for interpretation. One of the downsides, however, is that the setting can be a bit intimidating. Thus the committee might not learn as much about the candidate as they would have learned had they split into smaller groups for interviewing, using the round-robin approach.

Interview by Round-Robin Approach

In a previous chapter I gave the example of the CEO candidate (who ultimately got the job) feeling as if he were a commodity because the interview team brought three candidates in at the same time. The ideal situation might be to do as the candidate suggested and take three days to interview three candidates. However, my experience has been that committee members do not have the time to do this. That is why we started using a round-robin format. If the committee chooses to split into groups, questions can be divided between each group, giving them time for deeper exploration of the topics they have been assigned. For example, let's assume that in your particular situation the three primary functional responsibilities of your CEO are the following: fundraising, recruiting and building a team-based staff, and government relations.

Let's also assume that there are nine members on your search committee. Using the round-robin approach, you would divide into three groups of three. Each group would take one of the above functional areas and spend the bulk of their time exploring the candidate's level of experience in that area. The round-robin approach works particularly well when there are multiple candidates. If there were three

candidates, each team would take a topic, and your day would look something like this:

9:00 to 11:00 am	Government Relations—Candidate #1
	Fundraising—Candidate #2
	Recruiting and Building a Team-Based Staff—Candidate #3
11:15 to 12:15	lunch
12:30 to 2:30 pm	Government Relations—Candidate #2
	Fundraising—Candidate #3
	Recruiting and Building a Team-Based Staff—Candidate #1
3:00 to 5:00 pm	Government Relations—Candidate #3
	Fundraising—Candidate #1
	Recruiting and Building a Team-Based Staff—Candidate #2
6:30 pm	working dinner to discuss impressions and comments

One possible downside to this format is that since each group is asking somewhat different questions, the members of the other groups will have to rely on each other's reports. Another downside is that this method definitely takes more time. Both candidates and interview team members can be exhausted by the end of the day.

An advantage to this method of interviewing, however, is that members of the search committee get "three different looks" at the candidates. In one of our recent searches, the client used this manner of interviewing and liked it a great deal. They enjoyed that they collectively spent more than six hours with each of the candidates. Another strength they cited was that one of the candidates was flat with one group but had a strong interview with the other two groups. This enabled them to see more than one side of the candidate.

Should You Debrief Between Round-Robin Interviews?

When using the round-robin format, there will be a tendency for the team captains to debrief with each other between interviews. As with most things, there are pros and cons to each side of the argument.

On a positive note, debriefing between interviews can help the next interview team sharpen their focus. Let's say that Team One found an area that they really wanted to probe but ran out of time. If Team Two knows this ahead of time, they might rearrange their questions to allow for probing in the area of Team One's interest.

A possible downside to debriefing between interviews is that one team captain can have undue influence on another. I have seen a situation in which one captain virtually eliminated a very deserving candidate from consideration because his influence was so strong that he intimidated another captain.

In no way do I counsel against debriefing between interviews. I only caution board members to be aware that some of your peers can occasionally misuse their influence and cost you a fair look at good candidates. Additionally, if not used for debriefing, the time used between interviews can be used for gathering your thoughts, jotting down a few notes, and preparing for the next interview.

This day (or days) of interviews can be a time-consuming and emotionally draining process. Pace yourself, and realize how important it is to select the right candidate. The choice between having the committee, as a whole, interview each candidate or utilizing the round-robin format is up the committee. I prefer the round-robin format, but some of my committees prefer having the committee as a whole participate in the interview. Either way, you will get more meaningful and useful data if you use behavioral interviewing.

Be Yourselves...

We learned that leaders need all four qualities to be truly inspirational...the four leadership qualities are a necessary first step. Taken together, they tell executives to be authentic.

As we counsel the executives we coach,

"Be yourselves – more – with skill."

Robert Goffee and Gareth Jones

Making the Decision

12

HIGHLIGHTS

> **Honor the process**

> **Evaluating the data**

> **Making the decision**

> **What to do when you can't decide**

Hopefully throughout this search you have been using a deliberate process and not rushing. After you have interviewed the candidates (perhaps some of them twice) it is time to make your decision. This is not the time to change your tactics.

HONOR THE PROCESS

You have spent a considerable amount of time dedicating yourself to this search. Now that you're ready to make your decision as to which candidate you should hire, use the documents you've created to help you along the way—this will ensure you make the best choice in your new hire.

Review the CPRs

At the beginning of the process, you developed some specific selection criteria called the Critical Position Requirements. Now is a good time to review your CPRs again. Remember that a significant aspect of making a good decision is in determining how well the candidates compare to the selection criteria.

Use Your Search Committee

It is important that each member of the search committee has the opportunity to give input into the decision-making process. I have found it helpful to intentionally give each member of the search committee time to give her input on each candidate to the group.

Depending on how you have handled the checking of the references, this is a good time to review what each has said about the candidates. If the references were submitted in written form, take time to reflect upon what was said. If the references were checked by the individual members of the search committee, this is a good time for a round table discussion of what was learned about each candidate.

Beware of the Smile Factor

Remember that the person who gave the best interview might not be the best person for the job. You are hiring someone to provide leadership for the organization, not to be a professional interviewer. Don't be swept away by the person who "looks and acts the part." You are looking for the person who can do the job in the manner that you set forth in the CPRs.

Beware of the Smile Factor . . . the person who gave the best interview might not be the best person for the job.

This is where behavioral interviewing pays off. If you were diligent in the interview process to probe into "how the candidate did what she did," you will have substantial evidence as to whether she will do the job that you want done and in the manner in which you want it done.

EVALUATING THE DATA

By this time you have several sources of data. You need to take it all into consideration as you make your decision.

Resume and Application Package

In the searches that I lead, I require all of the applicants to submit an application package. This includes their resume, a list of references, and their written responses to a set of essay questions (unique to each search) designed to go beyond their resume. The essay questions for each search are usually different, depending upon what the search committee wants to know. You might be surprised what you can learn about a candidate by thoroughly reviewing their application package.

Reference Data

In addition to the references I have checked when formulating my short list, I ask the client to participate in further reference checking. I typically break the search committee into groups and they check two to three references on each candidate. I also check a couple of additional references for each person in the pool. We take good notes during the phone conversations and share what we have learned with each other.

Members of Search Committee should participate in the reference checking.

Recently I had an experience that put a different twist on the client participating in the reference checking. The search was for a university president. There was one person who had recently retired as a vice president, after being at the university for 20 years. She had the reputation of making excellent hiring decisions. It was known among the faculty and staff that if a new hire got through her reference checking, it was a solid hire. She was not on the search committee, but the chairman of the search committee floated the idea to the search committee that this woman be brought into the search process, specifically to check references. That is all she did and she did an outstanding job. Other members of the committee also participated in checking the references, but she led the way.

131

Interview Data

Obviously you will be interested in how the candidate performs in the interview. These questions will help you formulate a more solid opinion:

> What kind of impression did she make?
> Did his interview performance line up with his application package?
> Did she come across as competent?
> What did you learn from the interview about his oral communication skills?

Personal Chemistry

In addition to the candidate's technical abilities, you want to ensure that he will work well with your board and others in your organization. The following questions address issues of chemistry:

> Did you like the person?
> Would you enjoy working with or for this person?
> How well do you think the candidate would relate with your donor base?
> What did you learn about his interpersonal relationship skills?

Motivated Abilities Pattern

In my searches I use the System for Identifying Motivated Abilities© to compare the candidate with our Critical Position Requirements. (Refer to Chapter 7 for a refresher on Motivated Abilities Patterns.) This gives me an objective look at the candidate and how he will perform in the job of chief executive officer.

MAKING THE DECISION

As the search committee closes in on making their decision, they should be looking for positive alignment or congruence between all that they have learned about the candidate from his resume and application package, interview data, reference data, and comparison to the organization's CPRs. When this happens, the search committee can have more confidence in their decision. Once you think you have found a congruence in your desires for skills, style, and substance, it's time to take a vote! Here are several ways you can go about that:

Secret Ballot

Each search committee will vary on how to vote. My personal experience has been that it is best to vote by secret ballot. The primary reason is that this gives each person on the search committee the chance to vote their conscience without the possibility of being intimidated by another member. You would like to think that after working together for many months on this important decision that the committee would be past this possibility. However, there are usually still people who might feel intimidated, and the secret ballot will expedite the decision making process.

How Long Does It Take?

I have seen committees vote unanimously on the first round of ballots, and I have sat around the table with search committees for several hours as they have debated and discussed the merits of each candidate until they reached a decision. This is not the time to hurry. Remember: let the process work.

WHAT TO DO WHEN YOU CAN'T DECIDE

What should you do if you reach the end of the decision-making meeting and are not able to reach consensus on the candidate? Although I have never personally experienced this, I have heard that it does happen. If you should find yourself in this situation, you have a couple of options:

Start the Search Over

At the beginning of every search I tell my clients that I want them to be enthusiastic about the person they select for their next chief executive officer. My goal is for them to "select" a candidate, not "settle" on one.

Accept a Compromise Candidate

Very infrequently I have seen a committee that just could not come together around one candidate. This usually happens when there is not consensus on what the committee was really looking for in their next chief executive officer.

In most of these cases, the committee ended up split between two candidates. They usually revisited the short list and found the next best candidate—someone that both groups could agree on.

In conclusion, this is the time in the search process that you have all been waiting for. Short of having to settle for a compromise candidate, you have now selected the person who is your top choice for your next chief executive officer and are ready to celebrate! Before you sit back and relax, though, you first need to make the offer and get an acceptance.

The Offer

13

HIGHLIGHTS

> **Terms of employment**

> **Salary**

> **Who should make the offer?**

> **The offer and the counter offer**

> **How long should you allow for a decision?**

> **Notifying the stakeholders and other constituents**

Once the decision has been made as to which candidate you would like to hire as your next chief executive officer, the next step is to extend the written offer. A written offer accomplishes a couple of things:

> It enhances the professional atmosphere and thus reinforces the impression that you have been trying to make on the candidate.

> A well-written and comprehensive offer letter makes it easier for the candidate to respond to you.

It is best to make the offer letter as complete as possible by encompassing the suggestions in the following section. My co-author Bob Andringa has contributed a list of some terms of employment that you might want to consider including in your written offer.

TERMS OF EMPLOYMENT

Some not-for-profit boards negotiate contracts with their chief executive officers. Others have more informal memoranda of agreements. I firmly believe that the best time to clarify expectations and compensation is before the chief executive officer is hired. Annual reviews provide another time to clarify in writing any items that either the chief executive officer or the board wish to clarify. (I discuss annual reviews further in Chapter 15.)

Since the options for compensation are many, I typically recommend the board pay for the incoming chief executive officer to get independent advice from a financial advisor for his specific family needs, and then reach a mutual agreement with the candidate on the best package. Following is a list of the most common elements I have seen included in employment agreements. Depending upon the nature of your organization, not all of these may be applicable.

> Salary

> Normal fringe benefits available to all administrators, including pension benefits

> Term of employment (either open-ended or fixed, subject to formal extension)

> Vacation

> Provision for performance evaluations

> Housing or housing allowance (including house and grounds maintenance)

> Agreement on any needed redecoration of president's home

> Automobile or car allowance

> Entertainment and memberships

> Faculty tenure

> Sabbaticals

> Deferred compensation (normally as an incentive to stay longer than one otherwise might)

> Special insurance beyond other employees

> Travel expectations or limitations

> Treatment of honoraria, royalties

> Opportunity to consult with other organizations

> Spousal salary or honoraria for campus-related duties

> Home entertainment expenses for campus-related events

> President's discretionary fund for new programs

> Bridge loan if needed for the move to campus

> Compensation for costs of selling a house or moving expenses

> Tuition waiver or subsidy for children

> Delegation of responsibilities in case of severe illness

> Post-presidential responsibilities and opportunities

> Other matters important to the president or the institution

> Severance pay if involuntarily terminated

Having these items spelled out in writing makes your organization look more professional, offers less chance for miscommunication and misunderstanding later, and enables the candidate to know exactly what she can expect.

SALARY

As you can see from the above list, salary is only one component of the offer, albeit, for most people a very important component. In the late 1980s and early 1990s the discussion about salary in not-for-profit organizations might have centered on

excessive pay. Today it is more likely to center on where the organization is going to get the resources to pay the salary needed to attract the kind of leader they want.

I won't attempt to coach you on how much you should pay your chief executive officer, as the specific amount will vary for every organization, but rather offer a word of caution relative to the lack of privacy around this issue. If your organization is United States-based and incorporated, the salary of five highest-paid officers or managers are included on the IRS Form 990, an informational tax form that most not-for-profit organizations must file each year. This form is a public document that the organization must make available when requested by members of the public. Rest assured that if anyone wants to know how much your organization pays its top leaders, this information is readily available.

One positive about this is that this information is available to you when you are gathering data on how much to pay your chief executive officer. Web sites like www.guidestar.org are good places to go to do research on chief executive officer compensation for not-for-profit organizations. There are also associations and private firms that publish compensation survey results and firms that, for a fee, will conduct salary surveys specific to your need.

WHO SHOULD MAKE THE OFFER?

Should the offer of employment be made by someone on the search committee, or if you have a search firm assisting you, should the search consultant make the offer? On several occasions I have been asked to facilitate the offer on behalf of the client; however, it is more typical that a member of the search committee make the offer.

To a large extent this depends upon the comfort level and experience of the members of the search committee. If you have people on the search committee who are experienced in hiring senior level individuals, it is probably best for them to make the offer. Otherwise it is a good idea to ask for assistance.

THE OFFER AND THE COUNTER OFFER

Try as you might, it is sometimes difficult to compose the perfect offer letter on first attempt. There are often elements that are negotiable. If you have offered to pay for a financial advisor, you are more likely to have an offer that is on target. Unless you have had a very frank discussion with the candidate, you may not know what is most important to him, so don't be surprised or offended by a counter offer.

There should be someone on the search committee designated as the point person responsible for bringing this part of the negotiations to closure. If you are using a search firm, it can be a good idea to have the search consultant serve as the go-between here.

HOW LONG SHOULD YOU ALLOW FOR A DECISION?

Once you have extended the offer, how long should you give the candidate to decide? I'm not sure there is a "right" answer to this question, but I can say from experience that the longer it takes the candidate to make his decision, the greater the risk that he will not accept your offer.

The way to circumvent this is to have "pre-sold" his response. As you are developing a relationship with the candidate during the final evaluation process, do all you can to know whether he will accept your offer.

> **The longer it takes the candidate to make his decision, the greater the risk that he will not accept your offer.**

In one search I was down to two finalists. The plan was to have each of the finalists and their spouses back for a second interview prior to making the decision as to which one would get the offer. I encouraged the search committee to try to get a commitment from both of the finalists during the final interviews. Our plan was to

have the candidates spend a day at the organization's national headquarters. We finished with members of the search committee, as well as other members of the board who were local to the area, having dinner with each candidate and spouse.

After dinner the members of the board who were not on the search committee were dismissed, and the search committee finished the evening by answering any questions the candidates or spouses had. As that meeting drew to a close, one of the members of the search committee asked the candidate, "Based on what you have learned about our organization and the position, both during the interview process and from your time at the office today, do you know of any reason why you would not accept the position, if it is offered to you?"

In this case, both candidates responded that they would accept the position if offered. The members of the committee left the dinner meetings with a higher level of comfort, knowing that when the position was offered, it would likely be accepted. Three days later, the offer was made and accepted, with very little need for negotiation.

NOTIFYING THE STAKEHOLDERS
AND OTHER CONSTITUENTS

Now the celebration can begin. You have done all of the hard work, and your new chief executive officer has accepted your offer. You can send out your press releases and otherwise notify the stakeholders of your decision. In the midst of celebrating your new chief executive officer, don't forget to be thorough and strategic in breaking the news.

Stakeholders

Before you notify the public of your decision, you should contact the organization's key stakeholders: any board members, employees, key donors, and so on. Depending upon your timetable you can do this by letter or e-mail. Our experience has been that in recent years most of our client's stakeholders are regular users of e-mail. The effective use of e-mail greatly expedites this part of the process.

General Public

The selection of a new chief executive officer is a special time in the life of a not-for-profit organization. This is a good time for a press conference or some other public forum where you invite the media and present your new chief executive officer to the public. You should take this opportunity to get the most out of the announcement.

Successful Transitions

14

> **The Transition Committee**

> **Functions of the Transition Committee**

As the search draws to a close, there is a natural level of excitement about the new chief executive officer. In many cases, the search committee has been hard at work, putting in long hours to get your organization its new CEO. In your excitement about the future, do not forget that careful attention must be given to the transition between chief executive officers. This is particularly true when you have a long-standing chief executive officer who has served your organization well and is departing under normal circumstances. It is easy to place so much emphasis on the incoming chief executive officer that the outgoing leader can get a bad taste in his mouth.

Transition committees are often used to offset this type of situation. The reason the transition committee exists is to make sure that the outgoing leader has a smooth transition away from the organization and that the incoming leader has a smooth move into the organization. It has been Bob's experience, particularly in higher education, that the transition is more effective and less disruptive to all parties under the leadership of a committee such as this.

THE TRANSITION COMMITTEE

This committee should begin its responsibilities about three months prior to the incumbent's leaving office and continue for about three months after the new CEO has assumed her duties. Membership of the transition committee should be determined by someone on the board of directors, but at a minimum should include board members, key members of the organization, and key donors.

It is preferable for the transition committee to meet weekly. If the members are not all local to the area, or if some members happen to be traveling during the scheduled time for the meeting, they can meet by teleconference. It's important for the members to touch base frequently with each other as to how things are going.

FUNCTIONS OF THE TRANSITION COMMITTEE

Not only are the people who comprise the transition committee important, but the functions of the committee are critical to a smooth change in leadership. Here are some ideas on things they can do to make everyone feel appreciated:

For the Outgoing Chief Executive Officer

> Host a banquet in his and his family's honor. Celebrate him for the contribution he made to the success of your organization.

> Purchase an appropriate gift for her and her spouse. We heard of a recent instance in which the chief executive officer was given a pickup truck, and his spouse was given a nice diamond ring. In another instance, a CEO was building a new home in another state. The transition committee knew that his wife really liked the sculptures of a local artisan in the state to which they were moving, so they purchased one of these sculptures for their new home.

> If the chief executive officer is moving from housing that the organization has provided, offer to assist him with moving expenses.

For the Incoming Chief Executive Officer

> Make sure she has an ample travel budget if she has to make trips to the organization prior to taking office.

> If housing is provided, hire a decorator to work with the family to redecorate the home.

> Arrange meals or social occasions for him to get further acquainted with the members of the board and their spouses.

> Arrange meals or social occasions for her to get acquainted with her peers in the community.

The way an organization handles the transition from one chief executive officer to another truly reveals their class. They can choose to go out of their way for both parties and do their best to really make the new CEO feel welcome, or they can do little to nothing and run the risk of creating negative public relations from the transition. The amount of money that is spent during the transition is not the issue: it is the demonstration of gratitude from the heart that counts. Ensuring a smooth transition for the new chief executive officer of your organization helps to pave the way for his success in his new position.

The Board's Role in Evaluating the Chief Executive Officer

15

One day as I was driving to work I checked my voice mail and there was a message from the newly elected chairman of the board of trustees of a liberal arts college where I had just completed the search for their next president. He wanted to know if I could help him and the new president think about setting some first year performance goals. I have to admit that I had done several college president searches prior to this and had never been asked that question. It got me to thinking. Should assistance in that area be an integral part of our search process? Further conversations led me to give more thought to this matter and to ultimately address the issue here.

Now, our advice to prospective chief executive officers is this: Do not accept a position until you are sure of the criteria on which you will be evaluated and have the board's commitment to complete an annual evaluation with you. Otherwise, you may face the unhappy experience many chief executive officers have suffered—a surprise termination based on a difference of style with a few board members.

By the same token, I advise boards not to finalize their arrangement with a new chief executive officer without establishing the criteria upon which they will evaluate the performance of their chief executive officer. The best time to address these expectations is at the beginning, when every one is operating from a clean slate and there have been no disappointments.

INTRODUCING PERFORMANCE GOALS

A useful tool for allowing a board and its chief executive officer to reach mutual agreement on the CEO's focus for a given period of time is a list of performance goals. As a consultant who advises boards on matters of governance and policy, co-author Bob Andringa encourages boards and new chief executive officers to think about performance goals in the following manner. Depending upon the nature of your organization, all of these may not be applicable.

> ❯ There should be eight to ten performance goals *written* on one page.

> ❯ These should be S.M.A.R.T. goals. That is to say, the goals should be Specific, Measurable, Action-oriented, Realistic, and Timed.

> ❯ They should *reflect* at least 70 percent of the chief executive officer's time.

> ❯ They must help *fulfill* organizational goals and priorities set by the board.

> ❯ They are *negotiated* between officers and the chief executive officer; then the written document is approved by the full board.

> ❯ They are *changed* throughout the year, whenever the board *or* chief executive officer determines a need to do so.

> They are *specific,* so each can be *measured* to the extent practical.

> They are *referenced* in the chief executive officer's periodic reports to the board

> They are *reviewed* at the time of the board's annual evaluation of the chief executive officer, and then *rewritten* for the year ahead.

WHAT DO YOU EVALUATE?

The question "what do we evaluate?" can be answered in many different ways. Basically you want to evaluate all aspects of the CEO's *performance* in helping the organization accomplish what the board determined, within the board's policy guidelines. However, this is difficult to do if the board has not been clear in setting the organization's mission.

Here are some common questions board evaluation committees ask:

> Has the CEO built positive relationships with board members and helped strengthen the board?

> Has the CEO's leadership built a stronger internal organization in which systems, staff productivity and morale, and teamwork have improved?

> Has the CEO's leadership improved the quality and increased the quantity of the services we provide?

> Has the CEO's leadership increased the public's trust in our integrity?

> Has the CEO's leadership improved our financial resources and accountability?

The performance evaluation itself is improved when these elements are present:

> The CEO and the board know a year in advance what the performance goals are. Initiating this when the chief executive officer takes office is a great way to begin her administration.

> The chairman assigns two to three directors to take the lead in the evaluation.

> Once a year, the CEO is asked to give to the entire board his own written self-evaluation, tied mainly to the pre-agreed upon performance goals.

> All board members are invited to provide input related to the written goals, to the CEO's written self-assessment, or to their own concerns.

> Results are summarized and presented in both oral and written form to the CEO by not just one, but all the directors assigned.

> New written performance goals for the following year are negotiated between the CEO and the board, usually handled by the executive committee.

The performance goals should be more results-oriented than activity-oriented. For the chief executive officer, the board is not paying for hours worked but for achievements they agree are important to the mission of the organization.

AREAS TO EVALUATE

When there are clear goals *developed by the board*, the simple statement of performance is: Achieve the results envisioned in our goals through ethical, legal, and prudent leadership. Then the board evaluates how well the goals were achieved, based on reports, CEO self-assessment, observations, and so on.

Common categories for writing performance goals include:

> Board relations and development: board reports, strategic planning retreat, etc.

> Organizational development: staff restructure, training, technology updates, etc.

> Program results: X students achieved, Y new scholarship program reaches Z people, cooperative venture launched that accomplished X, etc.

> Finance: reserve fund reached X amount, investment policy adopted by board, new budget system adopted, X new sources of funding, Y total foundation grants, etc.

> External relations: joint venture signed with Y organization, articles on organization appeared in X publications, etc.

> Personal growth and leadership: attended workshop to learn X skill, kept travel calendar to goal of X nights away per month, etc.

MORE ON PERFORMANCE GOALS

Finally, good performance goals should be . . .

> Representative of that 50 to 60 percent of a CEO's time when he should be proactively leading, not just doing the routine work of the job

> "Owned" by both CEO and board through mutual negotiation

> Reviewed informally by the CEO and board a few times during the year

> Modified whenever the CEO or board feels it is justified

> Used as the point-of-reference for developing performance goals for those reporting to the CEO

> Shared with all staff, as appropriate, to help them appreciate why the CEO does what he does

> "Measurable" either by factual data collected and distributed to the board or by the board's own collective

judgment based on what members have seen or heard
from external constituents through the year and by
what they experienced personally in their volunteer
and governance roles with the organization

> The basis for the CEO's written and oral reports to
the board throughout the year

> The primary basis for the CEO's written self-evalua-
tion at the end of a year

> The basis for a results-oriented evaluation by the
board of its CEO, as opposed to making issues of
style or personality the focus of the evaluation

What if You Make a Mistake?

16

HIGHLIGHTS

> **The reputation of the organization**

> **Severance**

> **Confidentiality**

> **The organization is larger than the office of the chief executive officer**

Usually the days surrounding the hiring of your new chief executive officer are a happy time. A well-written, bubbly press release marks the beginning of a new chapter in the life of the organization. The great majority of the stakeholders are willing to give the new leader time to make his mark on the organization.

It isn't until the "new" chief executive officer is fired or resigns under a cloud of suspicion that the donors and other stakeholders get up in arms.

Philip R. Lochner Jr., in his article "Hiring, Firing, and CEO Succession Planning: The Board's Toughest Assignment," correctly sums up this situation:

> Hiring the right person for any task is an enormously difficult proposition. It is difficult to hire clerks and assembly line workers, much less CEOs. The important difference between hiring a clerk and hiring a CEO isn't that one job is easier to do than the other,

or that one is paid more than the other. It is that the cost of making the wrong decision is so much higher in one case than in the other.[6]

Lochner makes a good point. The cost of making a mistake at the executive level is high. This increases the criticality of the way you handle a mistake at this level.

THE REPUTATION OF THE ORGANIZATION

In the rare occasion when the results of the search do not bring the desired results, the best thing for your board to do is to admit the mistake, cut its losses, and move to find a new chief executive officer.

One of the main issues that your board must consider at a time like this is the organization's reputation. The way you handle a mistake at this level can have a big and possibly negative impact. The board needs to come together and reach a strategic consensus on how you will handle the resignation of the chief executive officer and how to communicate this to your internal and external publics.

Integrity

Handling the situation with the outgoing chief executive officer with integrity is the best policy: not always the easiest thing to do, but in the long run, by far the best way to get through a difficult time. This is not the time to "point fingers" or get back at anybody.

Transparency

Be as transparent as you legally can be about the details of the departure of the chief executive officer. This transparency needs to be in the light of doing your best not to further damage the reputation and credibility of the organization, the board, and the outgoing chief executive officer.

SEVERANCE

Except in highly unusual situations, don't pay the departing chief executive officer anything beyond what she is contractually entitled to. Being excessive in this area can bring down the ire of donors and other internal and external stakeholders.

Don't go overboard with your severance package.

CONFIDENTIALITY

Make sure that the outgoing chief executive officer is bound by confidentiality, non-compete, and no-raiding provisions. This is probably more pertinent in the private sector, but should not be overlooked in the not-for-profit sector. Agree on exactly who will say what to the press, donors, employees, and so on. In Chapter 13 I discussed what to include in the offer letter. Boards, obviously, do not expect to fire or otherwise remove their new chief executive officers from position early in his tenure, but it does happen. This is why it's important to include language about these circumstances when you negotiate the employment contract with the chief executive officer.

THE ORGANIZATION IS LARGER
THAN THE OFFICE OF THE CHIEF EXECUTIVE OFFICER

As painful as this unexpected change of leadership may be, the key point to remember is that the organization is larger than the office or title of chief executive officer. Making a mistake in this area is not the end of the world. Your organization will move past this and continue its mission.

At this point, the board will have to decide how to move forward. If the search process was long and draining, the members of the search committee may be emotionally and physically exhausted and not up to the challenge of conducting another search. In this case a new search committee will have to be formed. Although I have never seen it happen, the

board may reason that the previous search committee did not do a good job with the previous hire, so why should they be given the responsibility for a second time, and thus appoint a new search committee.

This is not the time to take sides and argue over what happened. It is the time for patience, wisdom, and discernment to prevail. As I stated in the title to this section, your organization is larger than the office of the Chief Executive. Be patient and keep moving forward.

Should You Use a Search Firm?

17

> The added value of using a search firm

> Arguments for using a search firm

> Arguments against using a search firm

THE ADDED VALUE OF USING A SEARCH FIRM

Every organization will need to determine for themselves whether or not to use a search firm when choosing their new CEO, basing their decision on the current state of their organization and board. While there are pros and cons to both sides of the argument—which I discuss in depth in the following sections—it's necessary to first look at three added values that a search firm provides.

Technical Know-How

A good executive search firm will bring technical know-how to the search. Along with this will come creativity and innovation. The search committee doesn't have to spend its time recreating and learning processes, but rather, they can spend more time dealing with the change that the organization is experiencing and understanding the specifics of what they are looking for in the next CEO.

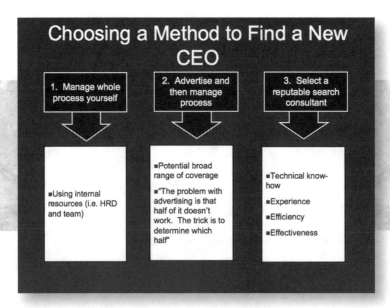

Experience

The problems you will face in your search are very similar to the problems other organizations face when they are looking for a new chief executive officer. These hurdles are not new to the search firm, and their experience will help you solve key problem more quickly. The right search firm will provide experienced senior staff to lead your committee.

Effectiveness and Efficiency

While your search will take some customizing, your problems and issues are generally the same as those a good search firm faces daily. You may be able to handle these problems and issues in time, but a search firm can likely deal with them more effectively and efficiently.

ARGUMENTS FOR USING A SEARCH FIRM

Since I make my living advising organizations on the selection of their senior executive leadership, I am obviously biased on this issue. You would question my integrity if I said otherwise! However, having stated my bias, I feel I have given a balanced perspective on the pros and cons of using outside counsel when conducting a search for a not-for-profit chief executive officer; the "cons" presented in the following section are based on input from friends and colleagues who have conducted successful searches without the aid of outside counsel.

Actually, it is my opinion that boards don't need a search firm if their organization can do what the search firm can do and do it as well as the search firm does it—that is to say, if the board has the time, talent, focus, and objectivity to devote to the project and if the level of sophistication required of candidates is not beyond that of committee members. Realistically, most boards are not in a position to dedicate these resources for the amount of time it takes to do a search correctly; consequently, in many cases it is best to hire an outside firm to direct your organization's search committee.

I have often observed boards get their searches off to good starts, but after a while the enthusiasm fizzles. One of

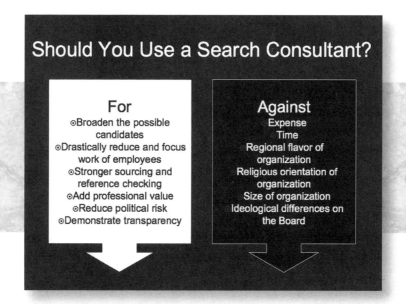

Should You Use a Search Consultant?

For	Against
⊙Broaden the possible candidates	Expense
⊙Drastically reduce and focus work of employees	Time
	Regional flavor of organization
⊙Stronger sourcing and reference checking	Religious orientation of organization
⊙Add professional value	Size of organization
⊙Reduce political risk	Ideological differences on the Board
⊙Demonstrate transparency	

the reasons for this is that the people who committed to the search process did not realize the time and energy commitment that they were making. Often they grow weary of the countless telephone calls, voice mail messages, missed calls, and so on. When this happens, the pace of the search slows to a crawl and the process slowly disintegrates. The tendency is to let the "easiest candidates"—friends (and friends of friends) of board members—become the pool of talent. There is nothing inherently wrong with these people; however, when your pool of talent is weighted in this direction, the overall quality of the pool decreases. A search firm, in contrast, brings dedicated time and energy to the search process.

To be more specific, the proper use of outside consultants can:

Broaden Your Network

When a board conducts their own search, they usually find themselves talking to their limited network of contacts to job candidates. They often will not take the time to get on the phone and "till the soil" until they have uncovered new people. In many cases, they will depend upon advertising rather than conducting focused research to identify a broad pool of candidates.

Drastically Reduce and Focus the Work of Employees

In addition to conducting the search process, someone has to manage and give direction to the search process. When a search firm is hired, the Search Committee only manages the search firm and not the entire search process.

Our experience has been that most members of search committees have not thought through the details that go into conducting a thorough search. It is easy to only think of the high points and ignore details like arranging the logistics for candidates to travel to interview, putting together a complete package on each of the finalists for each member of the search committee, and briefing or training the interview teams on the best way to conduct the interviews. The amount of time and attention that must be paid to detail is staggering.

Provide Stronger Sourcing and Reference Checking

A good search firm will check references as they go through the sourcing and qualifying phase of the search, particularly in high profile and high visibility searches. For example, when I am conducting a search for a college, university, or national nonprofit, and I have candidates who are regionally or nationally known, it is easy for me to ask questions like "Do you know John (or Jane) Doe? What would you think about him as the president of XYX University or XYZ Association?" Depending on their remarks, I can follow up with more questions designed to tell me more about why the person answered the way they did.

Add Professional Value to the Process

If you hire a good search firm, a principal or partner, who brings many years of experience in all aspects of the process, will be in charge of the search. She should lead in gaining a thorough understanding of the type of person who will thrive and excel in the position. She will bring years of interviewing and selection experience. Keep in mind that she does this full time. She spends more than fifty hours a week doing research, talking with people in her network, conducting telephone and face-to-face interviews, and applying her judgment in the selection process. The right search consultant will do most of the tasks related to the search process for you, which frees you up to concentrate on the reason you are serving on the committee to begin with—to make the decision about your next chief executive officer.

Reduce Political Risk

When a search is done internally, political problems can potentially arise. Unqualified friends of board members and others hear about the job and want to be considered. When you have to tell some of these people that they didn't make the short list, relationships can become damaged. There is also the danger of making a bad hiring decision if no one has the courage to eliminate some of these people along the way.

The search consultant works with you to minimize the risks, identify the unknowns, and put the odds in your favor.

The beauty of having a third party handle the search is that all these names can be passed along and evaluated along with the group of candidates that the search firm uncovers. By putting all candidates through this filter, only the most highly qualified make it to the short list. The search consultant works with you to minimize the risks, identify the unknowns, and put the odds in your favor.

ARGUMENTS AGAINST USING A SEARCH FIRM

Search firms do not place the great majority of chief executive officers, so there must be some truth to the fact that every vacant chief executive officer slot does not justify the use of a search firm. Often I will receive a call from a member of a not-for-profit search committee. The purpose of the call will be to explore the pros and cons of using a search firm. About half the time, after talking with me and a couple of other firms, the committee will decide not to use outside counsel and do the search themselves. There are many reasons for this.

Expense Too Great for Size of the Organization

Some people view the expenses associated with hiring a search firm as a poor use of the organization's resources. This is particularly true if the organization is small and has a small budget. (Typically, a full-retainer search firm will charge 30 to

35 percent of the CEO's first year compensation, plus out-of-pocket expenses.) I have talked with search committee members of small organizations and told them that while I thought I could add value to their search process, I knew that their resources were scarce. I also knew that there would be opposition from several of the organization's constituents. In these cases I will suggest that the organization hire me in a more limited capacity.

Requires Too Much Time

When I start a search I often tell my client that our process will take time. We view the time that we take, particularly on the front end of the search, as an investment in the ultimate outcome, while others may see it as time that could be spent advertising and networking for candidates. Depending on one's perspective, the use of a search firm can take more time than is necessary and thus be viewed as a waste of time.

Hurts Regional Context
of the Organization

Some not-for-profit organizations are regional when it comes to their scope, name recognition, and influence. Many search committees think that because of this, they can do a better, and perhaps quicker, job of identifying possible candidates. There will be members who believe that the use of a consulting firm will make the search impersonal and be a turn-off to some of the high-quality candidates who might respond to an inquiry from a local civic leader.

Unnecessary, Due to Religious
Orientation of the Organization

I have been approached by religious organizations with very specific doctrinal or theological persuasions. Because of this,

there is a limited number of people who would qualify for leadership positions in these organizations. Qualified candidates are usually well known within the support base of these organizations, and some members of the search committee would view the expense of using a search firm as a waste of financial resources when many candidates are already known.

Disruption Due to Lack of Consensus

If you press me, I can offer a counter argument for each of the four areas addressed above. However, when it comes to a board's lack of consensus about using a search firm, I have learned the hard way that it is best not to engage outside counsel.

If a search committee engages a search firm when there is not total agreement among the search committee members that this is a good idea, they are asking for trouble. The search firm feels the tension; lines are drawn, which makes the decision-making process more difficult, and goodwill and harmony seem to fall by the wayside.

Usually a search firm will not know about the lack of consensus until after the search has begun. If we were made aware beforehand, most of us would not agree to take on a search under these conditions.

Here are some specific things I have seen happen in a search when there is lack of consensus about using outside counsel:

> Members of the search committee bicker among themselves and to other constituents of the organization. This causes ill will and a lack of good internal, and occasionally external, public relations.

> On one occasion members of a search committee who were not in favor of using outside counsel actually sabotaged the search. These people deliberately went about destroying the credibility of the short list of candidates.

> Even if the search is ultimately successful, the infighting among members of the search committee can increase the amount of time it takes to complete the search and will have a negative impact upon the new administration.

I will not accept a search where I do not believe that there is agreement among the search committee members that I can add value to their search process and ultimately make it significantly better than if they had done it themselves. Regardless of the potential income, it isn't worth it to me to work with people who are not of one accord around this issue.

How to Choose and Use a Search Consultant

18

> Roles a search consultant has to fill

> What you need to know

> Getting names of reputable search consultants

> Evaluating different firms

> Making the most of your search consultant

> What should you do?

ROLES A SEARCH CONSULTANT HAS TO FILL

As I reflect on my practice, I am aware of the multiplicity of roles I have to fulfill to help my clients find the best person to lead their organizations. At various times I am a:

Confidante: Someone whom they can share their hopes and fears with, who can provide the reassurance they need that there *is* a solution to their leadership problem.

Process Creator: Someone who can create an effective process for finding and securing the best candidate for the job.

Resource Investigator: Someone who is mandated to find the best candidate for the job.

People Expert: Someone who knows how to assess people's strengths, discern their motives, and characterize their competencies.

Process Driver: Someone who will ensure that intent moves to action and that good ideas get followed through to practical outcomes.

Decision Facilitator: Someone with the best interests of the organization at heart and the objectivity to enable the board to do its job and choose the right candidate.

Midwife: Someone who enables the "new" to emerge—the birth of a new future for the organization.

Guarantor: Someone who ensures that a good process will lead to a good outcome.

Before you hire outside counsel to assist you in the search process, you need to know what you want from their help. What are your expectations? What can this firm or person do better or more timely than the search committee can do themselves?

If you have a good understanding of your expectations, better still, if you have committed these expectations to writing, you are in a much better position to look for and evaluate possible search firms.

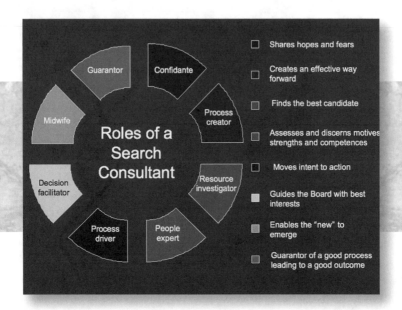

WHAT YOU NEED TO KNOW

It almost goes without saying, but nevertheless you should only hire a firm with a good reputation, integrity, and a strong track record of conducting searches for your type of organization. I won't elaborate on these qualities; however there are two questions you'll want to ask your consultant that might not be as obvious.

Who is Going to do the Work?

It is critical that you know who from the firm is going to actually conduct the search and that you meet this person and are comfortable with him or her. If you are not careful, you can fall prey to a search firm in which the "rainmakers" represent the organization and sell you on their services while your actual search may be conducted by other staff members.

There is nothing inherently wrong with a lower-level staff member conducting the search. In some cases, this person might actually spend more time on the project than one of the principals of the firm! Just make sure you know who will actually be representing your organization in the search process. This is of particular importance where your organization has a well-defined and adhered-to set of values.

Do We Have Values Coherence?

Most nonprofit organizations have a specific set of values. Religious organizations might have one set while social service organizations might have a different one. Make sure that the individuals who will be doing the actual work are people who are in agreement with the values you stand for and can effectively represent your organization to possible candidates.

GETTING NAMES OF REPUTABLE SEARCH CONSULTANTS

If your board is typical, your members are well connected, serving on other boards or knowing people who serve on the

boards of organizations similar to your nonprofit. These relationships are helpful as you assemble a list of possible search firms your organization can use in conducting your search. So where do you start in looking for recommendations?

> Ask friends or industry peers.

> Ask board members of similar nonprofits.

> Look in the Kennedy Directory of Executive Recruiters (http://www.kennedyinfo.com/js/ der.html) or other industry directories.

Using a directory is a rather mechanical way of gathering data. From a directory you can expect contact information such as company name, address, telephone number, e-mail address, industry or functional specialty, and so on. To get really meaningful input, you need to talk with someone who has actually used this firm or has fairly close knowledge of the quality of the firm's work.

This is where networking with friends or members of other nonprofit boards will be very helpful. Talking with these people

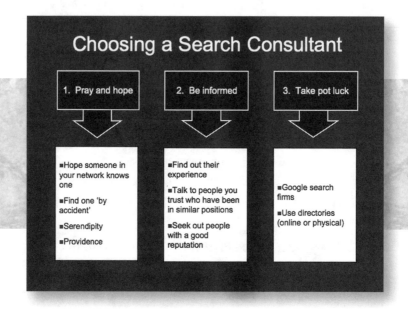

and getting first-hand knowledge of their experience with the various firms will help you decide which one is best for you. Let me illustrate. We may read a review on a movie or book and think we want to see the movie or read the book. However, if a friend who has seen the movie or read the book tells us about it, we are more prone to take action.

EVALUATING DIFFERENT FIRMS

When you have a short list (three to five candidates) of search firms that you want to consider, contact each of them and ask for a proposal. The proposals will usually contain a list of references. Telephone some of the references and discuss their experiences with the firm. When checking these references make sure the person who will be conducting your search is the same person who conducted the search for the reference organization. This is critical because you need specific information on the *person* who will be conducting your search as well as the *firm*. After you review the various proposals and checked their references, pick two or three firms to pursue further.

Some search committees prefer to have a conference call with the person in the search firm who will conduct their search. As a search consultant I have found this a good way to interact with a prospective search committee.

Sometimes search committees will assign different firms to individual members of the search committee and ask those members to meet with the consultant and report back to the committee.

Between these two methods, the conference call seems to work best. Having all the members of the search participate in a conference call gives everyone the same opportunity to interact with the consultant rather than depending on summary information from a third party, even if that third party is a member of your search committee.

Recently I received a telephone call from a person who had been asked to evaluate my experience. He was a bit

concerned about reporting back to the committee because his strength was not communication. His fear was that the committee might make a wrong decision because they would base their decision on the persuasiveness of the search committee member's communication skills and presentation, rather than truly understanding the pros and cons of each firm they were considering.

MAKING THE MOST OF YOUR SEARCH CONSULTANT

Should you decide to use a search firm, you have several options on how to best utilize their services. Over the past several years I have worked with some search committees who have been very creative and productive in utilizing our services. The best searches happen when the leadership of the search committee sits down with the search firm prior to beginning the search and brainstorms ways to get the most out of all involved parties.

Quarterback or Facilitator:
What is Your Preference?

Would you rather the search firm play a central role, running the search and making progress reports to you at stated intervals along the way? Or do you want the search firm to coordinate and facilitate the process but allow the search committee to have a very participative role throughout?

In many academic searches (those for a college or university president), I have worked with search committees who wanted to have regular, usually monthly, meetings at which the search consultants updated them of all that was going on in the search. These were working meetings. The search committee played a vital role in deciding which candidates remained in the pool of consideration. By working this way the search committee plays an active role in determining the composition of the short list.

WHAT SHOULD YOU DO?

There is no single way to make the decision about which search firm to hire. A lot depends on how much of the work you want to do, how much time you have to do the work, the expertise you can bring to the search process and the political implications of doing the work yourself.

To help you make this decision, you might ask yourself the following questions?

> ❯ Which firm seemed to have the best chemistry with our committee?

> ❯ Which firm has the most experience working with organizations in our area of work and our size?

> ❯ Are you sure you met the people who will be doing the work for each firm? What did you think of them? Don't be caught up in falling victim to a strong sales person who is a rainmaker for the firm but does very little work on the searches.

> ❯ What did the references say about the firms?

Beware the
$1-per-Year Executive

The Baby Boomer generation is one of the first to have had the luxury of considering leaving their jobs early in life in order to go to work for a nonprofit or charity. One of the biggest influencers toward this way of thinking has been the book *Halftime* by Bob Buford. In *Halftime*, a book about mid-life career transitions, Buford focuses on the possibilities at this stage for revitalization, for catching new vision for living the second, most rewarding half of life. His premise is that the second half of life can be better than the first. Many executives and others who are at this point in their lives have taken Buford's challenge to heart. One of the results has been that more of these people are investigating a second career in the not-for-profit sector.

While there is certainly a large group of people with incredible business and organizational skills, a word of caution is on order. Make sure that if you bring one of these people into your organization, he is willing to work as hard as he will have to, to make a go of it with your organization. I have often observed that this is not the case.

I have had two significant experiences with "$1-per-Year Executives. One was good for the client. The other wasn't as successful.

First, the good news. We were conducting a CEO search for a large international organization. The pool of candidates had been strong; so strong that the search committee initially interviewed six candidates. They narrowed the pool to the top two candidates. One of these was an individual who had recently taken his company public and then sold to a

competitor. As is the case in most of these situations, the man realized a significant profit from the sale.

The search committee asked me to talk with the individual about how serious he was about the position. My approach to him was direct. I remember asking him if he was up to the challenge of working as hard as he would have to work to lead this organization. I encouraged him to think back on how hard he had had to work to take his company public. I asked him if he really wanted to work that hard, or harder again. My final challenge to him was, "Wouldn't you rather sit on this organization's board and make a significant financial contribution to them each year than be their CEO?" He responded that no one had ever been that direct with him about his future. He asked for a few days to think about it. After a week or so he came back and told me that if he was offered the position, he would accept it and work as hard for the organization as he had worked in the private sector. He was offered the job and today is doing a great job in leading that organization.

There was another situation that didn't turn out as well as this one. The executive had been fortunate enough to make a small fortune in the IPO of the brokerage house where he worked. He retired from the brokerage house at age forty-seven and decided that he wanted to work for a nonprofit. He learned of such an organization that needed his help. Through a series of events, I introduced him to the CEO of one of my client organizations. After meeting with the CEO he moved his family and began working for $1 per year. About eighteen months into the job he realized that he had retired from a demanding job that paid him very well only to work seventy hours a week for $1 per year.

It wasn't the money that was the issue, but rather the fact that one of the reasons he had retired was to spend more time with his wife and kids. He was putting in as many and often more hours with the nonprofit than he had been at the brokerage house. In the end he decided that it was in the best interest of the nonprofit and his family for him to remain on the board, but leave his job and be intentional about spending more time at home.

Certainly his intentions in accepting the job with the nonprofit were good. The organization needed someone with his experience. The glitch was that, in the grand scheme of things, he wasn't willing or able to work the demanding hours that most nonprofit leadership positions require.

Since then there have been several instances where I have had strong interest in a particular chief executive officer position from people who have enjoyed very successful and financially rewarding careers in the private sector and are considering a second career as a not-for-profit chief executive officer. If I believe that someone like this is a serious contender for a given position, I have very frank discussions about the realities of moving into this role. These discussions usually center on the following issues:

Given what the particular not-for-profit organization needs at this time in its lifecycle, do you think you have what it will take to move them forward? Have you taken the time to look at their particular needs and evaluate them against the skills and natural talent that made you so successful with your previous company?

Are you sure you want to work as hard at this position as you worked to make your last company as successful as it was? This is in no way trying to dissuade the person from the job, but I do believe that I am doing both the person and my client a big favor by helping the candidate deal with this matter. You would be surprised at the number of people who thank me for asking them that question. During these discussions I usually learn that the person is very involved with a small number of their favorite charities. This involvement is usually financial as well as advisory. Many people in this group really enjoy this advisory role and would not really like to relinquish it if they took on a fifty- to sixty-hour-per-week full-time leadership position with another organization.

Understand that I have no bias against businessmen or -women having a second career in not-for-profit leadership. Quite the contrary. However, the point I make with them is to seriously look at their life and make sure that they really want to sign up for another tour of duty where the hours are as long and the work is as hard as it can be in not-for-profit leadership.

Job Fit

One conceptual way to think about how well a person's Motivated Abilities match Critical Position Requirements (i.e., Job Fit) is to visualize two overlapping rectangles. See Figure 1.

Figure 1.

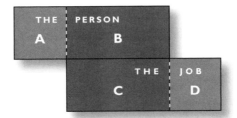

A. Underutilized Motivated Strengths

This is a good indication that the person has motivated strengths that are not required by the job. Every person has these. People often find ways to use these abilities outside of their paid work. Instances of this could be the hobbies the person has or some of the civic or volunteer work he does.

B. Motivated Abilities of the Person

This area of the rectangle represents the motivated abilities or motivated strengths of the person. Remember from Chapter 7 that motivated abilities are abilities that you never tire or get bored from using them.

C. Key Elements of the Job

This area of the rectangle represents the CPRs for success in the position.

D. Key Elements of the Job That Do Not Align with Motivated Strengths

This is the part of the job that calls for motivated abilities the person does not possess. I have never seen a job that was in total alignment with the employee's motivated abilities.

Overlap of B and C

I have seen occasions where the D part of the rectangle (i.e., the portion of the job that fell outside of the individual's motivated abilities) and the A part of the rectangle (i.e., the person's motivated abilities not used by the job) was very large. See Figure 2.

Figure 2.

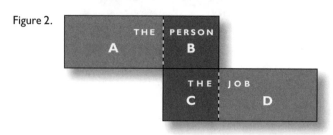

When considering a person for a particular position, you want to see a high degree of overlap between B and C. When this occurs there is the greatest chance for job satisfaction and success (as shown in Figure 1).

International
Boards

Our experience in this area has primarily been with large, international non-governmental organizations (NGOs); therefore, the perspectives presented here are more applicable to those types of boards. However, some of the information about culture and decision making might be helpful even in corporate settings where members are from non-western cultures.

Much of what I have written in this book is applicable to international settings. However, there will be cases where some of what is here may not apply due to cultural or legal realities.

Americans who are asked and choose to serve on a board that has strong representation from other countries, particularly developing nations, should realize that it will be a very different experience than serving on the board of a local not-for-profit such as a hospital, social service agency, church or charity in the USA.

Customs and methods are very different between cultures and societies. Asia and Africa and some Latin American cultures approach decision making and communications quite differently from their counterparts in the West. Let me emphasize that these comments are made by an American and should be kept in that light. There is also considerable literature on the differences between cultures in social interaction, communications and decision making, so some research could be very helpful in preparing to serve on an international board or to assist a search with an international board group.

In Asia, Africa, and some Latin American countries, decision making takes a "community" or consensus approach. It is generally true that these cultures place greater importance on relationships, mutual understanding, and consensus before making decisions or even progressing into meaningful dialogue. Meetings are frequently formal at the start. Be sensitive to the need to share about one's profession, community, organization represented, and possibly even family. This may seem "inefficient" to westerners, but engaging and enjoying this process will set the right tone. Europeans and North Americans tend to dive right into the data and choices with little relational process. Starting slowly, moving through the agenda, encouraging every member to contribute, and missing no one will yield better interactions. Spending greater time in the beginning of a meeting building trust and getting to know each other will usually make for a more productive process and better results in the end.

Mainly remember, be prepared to listen and exercise patience. As a rule, things don't happen as fast in these settings. People who are very "western" in their thinking and attitudes may get frustrated when things don't move quickly. Our advice is to schedule enough time and relax.

We westerners must to be open, patient and realize that just because values, politics and social approaches might be different that there is much can be gained as we adjust.

Having shared these observations, if you get the opportunity to serve on an international board, weigh your options, but serve if you can. You will learn a lot.

Sample
Documents

OPPORTUNITY PROFILE

Rather than include a specific example of an Opportunity Profile, the reader is encouraged to visit the Web sites of particular search firms that work in your specific niche along the not-for-profit spectrum. Many search firms (particularly the ones that conduct retained searches) will post Opportunity Profiles of their active searches on their Web sites.

CRITICAL POSITION REQUIREMENTS

I have included the Critical Position Requirements for chief executive officers of two very different not-for-profit organizations, which were at very different points in the lifecycles of their organizations. Pay particular attention to our note on the overall condition of the organization before reading the CPRs. As you read the CPRs, pay special attention to the action verbs that are in italics.

Case I

In this case, the client is a relief and development agency (NGO) that has recently created a strategic plan that calls for a significant increase in their annual fundraising goals.

The "organization" is ready for a new leader. The organization has been moving through a number of key changes and is now ready for a defined focus on the critical business of raising substantial funds to drive its mission and strategy.

Motivated strengths in strategic thinking, team leadership, implementation of strategy and action plans, board relations and leadership, an ability to collaborate as well as measurement of results against goals and expectations describe the right gifts.

While there are still some areas for role and responsibility clarification, the stage is set for a strong leader to establish the new foundation and set the course for significant growth and impact.

The ideal candidate should be gifted and motivated to:

Lead the implementation of the clarified role as the "engine" of fundraising for the network; *focus the resources* through the *development* of a workable strategy and measurable goals that define progress and success.

Raise large-scale financial resources from major donors, corporations, and foundations.

Build relationships with the large US board, establish personal ties and credibility, work closely to involve and manage individual personalities, expertise, and contacts, assuring each person's best overall contribution.

Realign and leverage the resources of the organization to focus on a five-fold increase in private dollars; *manage* the process of raising technical and government funds in complimentary ways, while assuring separateness required by the public sector.

Focus the resources of the organization on raising the funds; get results while experimenting with and refining the performance of the "machine."

Demonstrate adaptability in response to new funding opportunities, donor preferences, cultural or legal obstacles to standard organization products and approaches that are needed in a fast-changing worldwide network that operates in diverse national contexts.

Collaborate with the broader network leadership to accomplish results within a complex, multi-entity, matrix partnership that shares power, responsibility, and accountability.

Develop the marketing strategy that will propel the organization, clarify direction, and implement on the ground level through the fundraising team.

Motivate and catalyze others—board, employees, strategic partners and donors—to action and commitment.

Persuasively communicate across the spectrum from large-group presentations to one-on-one, personal calls.

Act as an adaptable and enthusiastic influencer, who can change the environment with the application of personal presence and "ask for the order."

Connect the passion and mission of the organization to every task, presentation, and situation, making the mission "live."

Case 2

The client is a healthcare organization that was losing $6 million per month at the time of the transition.

The ideal candidate should be motivated to:

› *Build* and, in many cases, *rebuild* relationships of trust with physicians, trustees, community and business leaders and senior managers in both the xxxxxxx System and xxxxxxx Hospital, who have lost confidence in the organization's ability to make good on promises.

› *Lead the turn around* of xxxxxxx Health, building a foundation of vision, values and financial performance that will assure growth and results.

› *Develop the clarity of purpose* needed to be successful in the xxxxxxx market; redesign and then persuade others to accept a new vision of usefulness and contribution making partnership real.

› *Manage collaboratively, build the team* and *provide very clear expectations* to assure accountability to the organization and its management at all levels.

› *Set goals and direction, anticipating* and *avoiding* the obstructions and pitfalls; *develop a plan* for xxxxxxx Health that takes "the level playing field" idea into account and get acceptance for the plan from xxxxxxx Health shareholders.

› *Make decisions* using objective data and do not alter direction or strategy without the confirmation of real information.

› *Communicate openly* and *demonstrate a commitment to listen, understand* and then *act*; be clear and do not "mince" words.

› Integrate, where appropriate, with xxxxxxx Health System and xxxxxxx Hospital programs but *defend the redesigned vision and direction*, bring the clarity that is absolutely necessary for performance.

> Focus and direct medical, marketing, financial, information systems, human and operating resources to *consistent and effective performance; get measurable results*.

> *Demonstrate political savvy*, finding the common ground among often competing interests, personalities and organization entities.

Action and Reflection

Given the stark reality of the difference between the financial condition of the university in Case 1 and the healthcare organization in Case 2, what is different about the Critical Position Requirements?

THE PERFECT
SEARCH

MISCONDUCT SELF-CERTIFICATION
STATEMENT

Not-for-profit organizations use a variety of language in their Misconduct Self-Certification Statements. In the world of churches and/or denominations, they also vary.

In no way are the authors offering legal counsel here or anywhere else in this book.

You should consult your legal counsel before writing or using a Misconduct Self-Certification Statement.

Some of the statements that we have seen usually have language relating to some of the following areas:

The person signing the document certifies that

> No civil, criminal, or ecclesiastical complaint has ever been sustained or is pending against him/her for misconduct (i.e., ethical, sexual, etc.).

> S/he has never resigned nor been terminated from a position for reasons related to misconduct or any other inappropriate conduct.

> There is no fact or circumstance involving him/her that will call into question neither his/her ethical or moral judgment nor anything that would or could cause embarrassment to this organization.

Some documents insist that the applicant sign a release form that stating that the information obtained may be used to deny their employment or any other type of position from the employing entity.

SEARCH COMMITTEE
APPOINTMENT AGREEMENT

The idea behind the Search Committee Appointment Agreement is that the person joining the committee realize the importance of the work of the committee and that it will take time away from his/her already busy schedule. Obviously this is not a legally binding agreement, but just the fact that it is in writing and the person signs the document adds to the level of commitment that s/he is making.

Your Search Committee Appointment Agreement should include language similar to that below. The more specifics you can put in the agreement the better.

> If you have a pre-determined schedule of meetings (date and time), include this.
> If you know the start date of the search and target completion date, include this.
> If you know that there will be out of town or overnight travel involved, include this.

Following is some suggest language to get you started.

I am honored to be asked to serve on the search committee for the Chief Executive Officer of [name] organization. I realize that the work of this committee is very important and could very well be the most important decision or input that the Board of Directors has to the future of [name] organization.

I realize that this is a significant commitment; particularly as it relates to my schedule. I realize that I will be involved in frequent meetings (monthly in the beginning, and more frequent as the search progresses).

I realize that when the interviews begin, I will be required to participate. These meetings could be day long sessions. There could be more than one session.

I commit to do everything possible to give my undivided attention to the work of this committee.

_____

Signature
SEARCH COMMITTEE MEMBER

_____

Signature
CHAIRPERSON OF SEARCH
COMMITTEE

_____

Date

_____

Date

Notes

1. Rath, Tom, *Strengths Finder* (2.0 Gallup Press, 2007).

2. Collins, Jim, *Good to Great* (New York: HarperCollins, 2001).

3. *Fund Raising Management* 32:5 (July 2001), 42.

4. The material in this chapter draws heavily on content written by my colleagues at People Management International LLC, especially the book *Passion and Purpose: How To Identify and Leverage the Powerful Patterns That Impact Your Work/Life*, by Marlys Hanson, M.S. with Merle Hanson, Ph.D., Pathfinder Press, 2002. The preface to *Passion and Purpose*, from which I have extracted, was written by Dr. Arthur F. Miller. Jr., the developer of the SIMA© methodology and founder of People Management International LLC. *Passion and Purpose*, available on www.amazon.com, provides readers with self-guided analysis of their motivations and assistance in defining "best use" of their giftedness.

5. *HR Magazine* 39:9 (Sept. 1994), 54-55.

6. Phillip R. Lochner Jr., *Directorship* 25:11 (Dec. 1999), 4-5.

Index

Notes

Notes

Notes

Notes

Notes

Notes

Notes

Notes

Notes